Dashulia,

♡ I want you to read this little BOOK Over and Over and Over....! With your friends, family, coworkers, strangers

ULTIMATE

BOOK OF

JOKES

I feel that when you laugh, you Enjoy and live _that_ Present Moment. You forget about any problems in life... Even is its just for a minute! Everything gets Better and Brighter... Laughing makes you feel Happy, Silly, Healthy, Young, Alive !!!

"To Laugh often and much; to win the respect of intelligent people and the affection of children; to earn the appreciation of honest critics and endure the betrayal of false friends; to appreciate beauty; to find the best in others; to leave the world a bit better, whether by healthy child, a garden patch or redeemed social condition; to know even one life has breathe'd easier because you have lived. This is to have succeeded."

Ralf Waldo Emerson

"ULTIMATE"

BOOK OF

JOKES

The Essential Collection

OF MORE THAN 1,500 JOKES

BY SCOTT McNEELY

ILLUSTRATIONS BY ARTHUR MOUNT

CHRONICLE BOOKS
SAN FRANCISCO

Text copyright © 2011 by Scott McNeely.
Illustrations copyright © 2011 by Arthur Mount.

Library of Congress Cataloging-in-Publication Data

McNeely, Scott.
 Ultimate book of jokes / Scott McNeely.
     p. cm.
 ISBN 978-0-8118-7795-4 (hardcover)
 1. American wit and humor. I. Title.
 PN6165.M45 2011
 818'.602—dc22

                        2011005324

Manufactured in China

Designed by Warmbo Design

10 9 8 7 6 5

Chronicle Books
680 Second Street
San Francisco, CA 94107

www.chroniclebooks.com

DEDICATION

This book is dedicated to Emmett, Hollis, and especially Aimee, who reminded me frequently that some people can tell a joke, and some people can't.

~

It's the first day in prison for a new convict. He's in his cell, talking to his new cellmate, when somebody yells "218." Suddenly the entire prison block bursts into laughter. A few minutes later somebody yells "92" and, again, the entire prison block bursts into laughter.

The new prisoner has no idea what's going on, so he asks his cellmate, "Hey, what's so funny about '218' and '92'?"

The cellmate explains, "There's only one book in the prison, and it's a joke book. We've all read it so many times we've memorized every joke. So now, we only have to hear the number to crack up laughing."

The new prisoner wants to prove his mettle, so he goes to the library and studies the joke book.

After a few weeks he's ready. Somebody yells "43" and the entire prison block bursts into laughter.

A minute later the new prisoner yells "189." There's a dead silence. "Hey, what just happened?" the new prisoner asks his cellmate. "Why didn't anybody laugh at my joke?"

"Well," the cellmate explains, "some people can tell a joke, and some people can't."

TABLE OF CONTENTS

Introduction

WHY DID I WRITE THE *ULTIMATE BOOK OF JOKES*? It's because most jokes books I've come across are emphatically *not* funny. And don't get me started on the pitiful state of humor on the Internet. Hey, Google! There's nothing amusing about listing page after page of look-alike Web sites peddling carbon-copy lists of mediocre jokes. (And a note to those copycat joke Web sites: If I wanted a free screensaver, I'd ask for one. A pox on your pop-up advertisements!)

Needless to say, I couldn't find a decent laugh anywhere. So I took matters into my own hands. I asked friends to send me their favorite jokes; many graciously complied. I scoured secondhand bookshops and mercilessly harangued colleagues, friends' children, and random people on the street, always on the hunt for laugh-inducing source material.

While I can't claim every joke in the *Ultimate Book of Jokes* rates a triple-chortle belly jiggle, I can promise this: You will laugh reading this book. And laugh often.

All I ask is one favor. Please don't read this book alone. In fact don't *read* this book at all! Since cavemen first cracked a smile at the foibles of others, joke telling has been an oral art. Jokes were rarely if ever written down. They were instead passed along by great storytellers, by performing artists and playwrights, and by bawdy uncles at family get-togethers.

Jokes are funniest when spoken aloud and shared. And that's my advice—use this book to share a few hearty laughs with family and friends.

You're also encouraged to take these jokes and make them your own. Jokes are not pieces of legislation passed by a congress and they are not messages from on high. Jokes are fluid things, and the best punch lines always reference current events and personalities. So by all means, tweak a detail here or there. Make these jokes suit your tastes and cultural references. Doing so is no crime; rather, it places you squarely in the tradition of court jester and stand-up comedian.

* * *

It's been said that nobody ever tells a joke for the first time. I do not claim any different. Each joke in this book has been around the block a few times because joke books are not written so much as they are curated. My job has been to sort the comedic wheat from the chaff, to polish language and sharpen punch lines, and to provide some historical perspective.

—SCOTT MCNEELY

CHAPTER

***** .01 *****

It's Important to Laugh

* * * * * * * * * * * * * * * * *

CHAPTER 1

It's Important to Laugh

JOSEPH ADDISON, A SEVENTEENTH-CENTURY ENGLISH WRITER, once said, "Man is distinguished from all other creatures by the faculty of laughter." And it's true, we humans are notable for the range and complexity of our humor. Wit, satire, sarcasm, irony, farce, slapstick—we find many ways to make ourselves laugh.

Of course, this marvelous capacity to laugh is often paired with subject matter that would make a whore blush: farts, bawdy plays on the word "cock," and ribaldry at the expense of alcoholics, men of the cloth, loose women, *and* midgets. Somehow we can make ourselves laugh at dead babies, blind people, Jews, Italians, Canadians, lawyers, and bubbas. No race or ethnicity is spared, no profession or hobby or character flaw escapes the spotlight. Jokes are the ultimate social equalizer.

Can jokes go too far? Can they hurt feelings? Absolutely. It's guaranteed that at least one joke in this book will offend you; it simply goes with the territory. Just remember that the events depicted in jokes are fictitious. Similarities to any persons living or dead are merely coincidental.

WHAT IS A JOKE?

What's the difference between a joke and a funny story? One of the big differences is the buildup to a punch line. Jokes have punch lines, funny stories usually don't.

Jokes are also mercifully short. Two or three lines are all you need for a joke to hit its target. And often jokes have a formulaic setup that hastens the climax (think: yo mama jokes, bar jokes, lightbulb jokes, knock knock jokes, etc.).

After you read a few thousand jokes, it's also clear that jokes fall into two broad categories that humans—no doubt since the dawn of time—have found irresistibly funny. The first is so-called situational humor where an incongruous situation or a false assumption prompts a howl of laughter. The hallmarks of these jokes are talking animals, wish-granting genies, and foul-mouthed priests. Whenever day-to-day reality is even slightly distorted, it's a golden opportunity for an unexpected—and unexpectedly funny—punch line.

The second category involves wordplay. Double entendres and clever turns of phrase are the hallmarks here. Late-night television hosts and stand-up comedians are the masters of this style of humor. Think of Johnny Carson, David Letterman, Jon Stewart, and Monty Python's merry pranksters.

Why do we laugh at jokes? Scientists and professors, theorists and folklorists, not to mention the bartender at your local bar, have all thought deeply about this question. No surprise then that there are many theories of laughter—how laughter relieves inhibition, how laughter allows us to metaphorically beat up our social superiors, how laughter gives us a mechanism for dealing with socially taboo subjects such as racism, addiction, infidelity, and death.

None other than Sigmund Freud argued that jokes, like dreams, are reflections of our unconscious desires and allow us to share publically our sexual, aggressive, and cynical tendencies (which otherwise remain locked away in our subconscious).

Fair enough. But that doesn't satisfy the question of why we *laugh* instead of simply clap when somebody tells a rip-roaring joke. One theory argues that laughing itself promotes a healthy immune system: people who laugh at jokes are more likely to endure life's vicissitudes better than humorless sticks-in-the-mud who rarely crack smiles. We laugh because it is healthy to laugh.

Believe it or not, a hearty laugh does exercise your heart (by increasing your heart rate) and tone muscles in the face and upper body. Think of laughing as a mini-workout for your body, mind, and spirit.

THE JOKE'S ON YOU

In 2001, Professor Richard Wiseman decided to answer the question, "What is the world's funniest joke?" He created the LaughLab Project (www.laughlab.co.uk) to investigate this age-old riddle using modern scientific methods. After more than 40,000 joke submissions and more than 1.5 million ratings from joke lovers around the world, Professor Wiseman had his answer. Without further ado, the world's funniest joke according to LaughLab:

Two hunters are out in the woods when one of them collapses. He doesn't seem to be breathing and his eyes are glazed. The other guy whips out his phone and calls emergency services. He gasps, "My friend is dead! What can I do?"

The operator says, "Calm down. I can help. First, let's make sure he's dead."

There is a silence, then a shot is heard. Back on the phone, the guy says, "Okay, now what?"

Unfortunately, it turns out the world's funniest joke is not very funny. It rates a chuckle, for sure (we all enjoy laughing at the antics of stupid people). Yet is it the funniest joke on planet Earth? Not by a long shot.

The problem is that most of us are not hunters. The culture of hunting is not part of our daily experience (apologies to the avid hunters reading this book). So the premise, while obviously humorous, feels distant. We're hearing a story about random people with whom we share few direct connections. And this points to a deeper truth

FUN FACT:
TIPS FOR BEING FUNNY

Most people assume you need a sense of humor and a knack for storytelling to make people laugh. The world's great joke tellers possess impeccable timing and an infectious belly laugh, to be sure. But according to the LaughLab Project, a handful of other attributes contribute to jokes being considered "funny":

❧ People found jokes funniest at 6:03 in the evening, the least funny at 1:30 in the morning.

❧ People found jokes funniest on the fifteenth of the month, less funny toward the end or start of the month.

❧ Jokes averaging 103 words are funniest.

❧ Many jokes poke fun at animals; those featuring ducks are funniest.

about jokes: the funny ones hit close to home. The funniest jokes leverage your own experiences, and often your own insecurities, to make a point.

For this reason there never can be a single "funniest" joke. What you find funny is always filtered through the prism of personal experience and cultural perspective.

AM I A SEXIST RACIST HATER FOR LAUGHING?

The thing about jokes is that there's inevitably a target or victim. Every joke has a butt. And *nobody* likes being a butt.

Knock knock. Who's there?

Yo mama.

Yo mama who?

Yo mama's a blonde redneck Catholic drunk who crossed the road to walk into a bar to have an affair with a fat, blind, Jewish-Italian, Republican, pot-smoking, lightbulb-changing lawyer who pleasures twelve-inch pianists.

Did anybody get left out? Hopefully not. It's in the very nature of jokes to throw salt on the wounds of people caught in their comedic nets. So the only chance of *not* being considered a sexist racist hater is to offend everybody.

Are jokes hurtful? Yes.

Is it okay to laugh? Yes.

What's not okay is telling a joke with the explicit intent to hurt somebody's feelings. And the only way to understand intent is to understand context. Is it okay to tell a blow job joke to your girlfriend's parents? Or a lawyer joke to a group of lawyers? What if Barack Obama told a Bill Clinton sex joke to Hillary? Or to Chelsea?

The very same joke can come across as hilariously funny, mean-spirited, harassing, or straight-up hateful. It all depends on how well you know your audience. And on how much your audience trusts your intentions. "Guns don't kill people," the saying goes, "people kill people." It's a similar story with jokes.

As with so many things in life, the Golden Rule comes in handy: joke unto others as you would have others joke unto you. Follow this simple advice and you'll always laugh with a clean conscience.

A VERY BRIEF HISTORY OF JOKE BOOKS

It's said that the world's oldest profession is prostitute and the second-oldest profession is politician. Perhaps the third-oldest profession is joke teller. References to jokes go back to the very beginning of written history.

The godfather of comedy is Crates, a fifth-century Greek playwright who penned the world's first one-liners. The ancient Greeks, in fact, were serious about their jokes. In Athens there was a comedians' club called the Group of Sixty that met regularly to trade wisecracks and funny stories (Philip of Macedon supposedly paid handsomely to have the group's jokes written down; if such a book ever existed, it's sadly been lost).

The Roman playwright Plautus refers to "books of jest" in his plays, and the Roman scholar Melissus is said to have authored more than a hundred joke anthologies. Unfortunately, there's only a single surviving example of these ancient joke books. The *Philogelos* (Laughter Lover) is a fifth-century AD collection of Greek jokes that, somewhat shockingly, still tickles the funny bone even today (for examples, see the "Ye Olde Guffaws" chapter).

Europe completely lost its sense of humor during the Dark Ages. Fortunately, the art of joke telling survived in the Arab world; over the course of the Crusades, the concept of written humor filtered slowly back into Western consciousness.

The rebirth, so to speak, of Western joke anthologies came in the late fourteenth century courtesy of an Italian, Poggio Bracciolini, secretary to eight early Renaissance popes. Bracciolini traveled across Europe searching for lost works of literature. Bracciolini is credited with salvaging priceless manuscripts by Cicero and Lucretius, and yet history remembers him mostly for his lone joke book, *Liber Facetiarum*. This short collection of jokes was the first of its kind to be published in Europe. When it hit the shelves in 1452, filled with political jokes and ribald tales of lusty church officials, it was an instant hit.

In Elizabethan England writers such as Christopher Marlowe, Francis Bacon, and William Shakespeare took the funny stories of past ages and transformed them, in printed form, into something that you'd instantly recognize as a joke. The hallmarks of Elizabethan humor are still with us today: wit, satire, double entendre, and the buildup to a punch line.

CHAPTER
***** .O2 *****

Blind, Lame & Dumb

* * * * * * * * * * * * * * * *

CHAPTER 2

Blind, Lame & Dumb

THE BLIND, THE LAME, AND THE DUMB—what a bunch of idiots.

Actually, it's hard to think of a group more deserving of empathy . . . which makes this chapter hard to stomach for joke lovers with weak constitutions. You're treading on thin comedic ice when the punch line to a joke about a blind, deaf, and mute quadriplegic is "Cancer"!

If you're feeling guilty, just remember—telling jokes about the blind, lame, and dumb is like shooting fish in a barrel. These folks can neither see you nor understand much of what you're saying. They are perfect targets.

So in their honor we kick off the *Ultimate Book of Jokes* poking fun at people who least deserve it, and who are the least equipped to protest. Bravo!

* * *

A young blind boy was being tucked into bed by his mother. His mom said, "Honey, I want you to pray really hard tonight so that tomorrow, your wishes will come true!"

The next morning the boy woke up and screamed, "Mommy! My wish didn't come true. I'm still blind!"

"I know," his mom replied. "April Fools!"

* * *

Q: Why did the boy fall off the swing?
A: He didn't have any arms.

Q: How many deaf people does it take to screw in a lightbulb?
A: None. They all just sit in the dark and cry.

Q: What's even better than winning the Special Olympics?
A: Not being a retard.

Q: How did the blind kid burn the side of his face?
A: He answered the iron.

Q: How did he burn the other side?
A: They called back.

Q: Why don't blind people skydive?
A: It scares the hell out of their dogs.

* * *

Q: Why did Helen Keller cross the road?
A: What, you think she has *any idea* where she is going?

Q: What did Helen Keller do when she fell down the stairs?
A: Screamed her hands off.

Q: Why was Helen Keller's leg yellow?
A: Her dog was blind, too.

Q: What did Helen Keller's parents do to punish her for swearing?
A: They washed her hands with soap.

Q: Why did Helen Keller's dog jump off the cliff?
A: You would, too, if your name was mmmmmmmnnnnnnnpf.

Q: Why were Helen Keller's hands purple?
A: She heard it through the grapevine.

Q: What does Helen Keller call her closet?
A: Disneyland!

Q: How did Helen Keller burn her hands?
A: Reading a waffle iron.

Q: What is Helen Keller's favorite color?
A: Corduroy.

Q: If Helen Keller fell down in the woods, would she make a sound?

Q: Why can't Helen Keller drive?
A: Because she's dead.

* * *

Two morons were walking through the woods and they came to some tracks. The first moron said, "These look like deer tracks."

The other moron said, "No, these look like moose tracks."

They argued and argued, and were still arguing when the train hit them.

* * *

A moron ordered a pizza and the clerk asked if he should cut it in six or twelve pieces. "Six, please. I could never eat twelve pieces."

Helen Keller was born in Alabama in 1880 and died in 1968 (*not* from reading a waffle iron). Despite being both deaf and blind, Helen learned to sign and became a prolific author, scholar, and antiwar protester.

While nobody knows who told the first joke about Helen Keller, by the early 1980s Helen Keller joke lists went viral thanks to the very first mass-market joke books such as *Truly Tasteless Jokes* (which hit the *New York Times* bestseller list, believe it or not).

* * *

Two morons walked toward each other on a country road. The first moron was carrying a burlap bag over his shoulder. "Hey, what's in the bag?"

"Chickens," the second moron replied.

"If I guess how many, can I have one?"

"Sure, you can have both of them."

"Okay. Five?"

* * *

Q: How do you get a moron out of a tree?
A: Wave.

Q: How do you make a moron laugh on Saturday?
A: Tell him a joke on Wednesday.

Q: Why do morons work seven days a week?
A: So you don't have to retrain them on Monday.

Q: Why did the moron hit his head against the wall?
A: Because it felt so good when he stopped.

* * *

Two morons are at a train station. The first moron asks the clerk, "Can I take this train to Chicago?"

"No," the clerk replies.

"Can I?" asks the other.

* * *

Q: What goes "Click-click-click . . . Did I get it?"
A: Stevie Wonder doing a Rubik's Cube.

Q: How did Stevie Wonder meet his wife?
A: Blind date.

Q: Why didn't Stevie Wonder like the cheese grater he got for Christmas?
A: Because it was the most violent book he'd ever read.

Q: What do you call a tennis match between Stevie Wonder and Helen Keller?
A: Endless love.

* * *

A blind man is sitting on a park bench. A rabbi sits down next to him eating a piece of matzoh. Taking pity on the blind man, the rabbi breaks off a piece and gives it to him. Several minutes later the blind man turns to the rabbi and asks, "Who wrote this crap?"

* * *

Q: What do you call a guy with no arms and no legs in a pile of leaves?
A: Russell.

Q: What do you call a guy with no arms and no legs in the ocean?
A: Bob.

Q: What do you call that same guy two weeks later?
A: Fish food.

Q: What do you call a guy with no arms and no legs in a forest fire?
A: Bernie.

Q: What do you call a guy with no arms and no legs hanging on the wall?
A: Art.

Q: What do you call a guy with no arms and no legs on your front steps?
A: Matt.

Q: What do you call a dog with no arms and no legs?
A: It doesn't matter, he won't come.

Q: What do you call a cat with no arms and no legs?
A: Dog food.

Q: What do you call a girl with one arm and one leg?
A: Eileen.

Q: What do you call a Chinese girl with one arm and one leg?
A: Irene.

Q: What do you call a girl with no arms and no legs sitting on a grill?
A: Patty.

Q: What do you call a guy with no arms and no legs sitting on a grill?
A: Frank.

Q: What do you call an electrician with no arms and no legs?
A: Sparky.

Q: What do you call a guy with no arms and no legs covered in oil?
A: Derek.

Q: What do you call a guy with no arms and no legs resting on a podium?
A: Mike.

Q: What do you call a guy with no arms and no legs on hot pavement?
A: Flip.

Q: What do you call a guy with no arms and no legs under a car?
A: Jack.

Q: What do you call two guys with no arms and no legs hanging from a window?
A: Curt and Rod.

Q: What do you call a guy with no arms and no legs in a tiger cage?
A: Claude.

Q: What do you call a guy with no arms and no legs in your mailbox?
A: Bill.

Q: What do you call a guy with no arms and no legs riding a roller coaster?
A: Ralph.

q: What do you call a girl with no arms and no legs who feels worthless?

a: Penny.

q: What do you call a guy with no arms and no legs covered in sauerkraut?

a: Reuben.

q: What do you call a girl with no arms and no legs on a tennis court?

a: Annette.

q: What do you call a guy with no arms and no legs on a golf course?

a: Chip.

q: What do you call a guy with no arms and no legs caught in a meat grinder?

a: Chuck.

* * *

A man was sitting in a bar and noticed a group of people using sign language. He also noticed the bartender was using sign language to speak with them. Curious, the man asked the bartender how he had learned sign language. The bartender explained that these were regular customers and had taught him to sign.

A few minutes later the man noticed that the people in the group were waving their hands around wildly. The bartender looked over and signed, "Now cut that out! I warned you!" then threw the group out of the bar.

The man asked why he had done that and the bartender said, "If I told them once I told them a hundred times—no singing in the damn bar!"

* * *

Frank and Tom were walking their dogs on a hot summer day and passed a bar that didn't allow pets. Tom said, "I sure wish we could go have a beer."

Frank thought for a minute and said, "Do what I do, and follow my lead." He put on his sunglasses and followed his German shepherd into the bar as if he were blind. Tom waited a minute. Frank didn't come back out, so Tom put his sunglasses on and followed his dog into the bar.

The bartender looked at them and said, "You can't bring that dog in here."

Tom protested, "But he's my seeing-eye dog."

The bartender scoffed and said, "Schnauzers aren't seeing-eye dogs."

Tom paused a moment and said, "Wait a minute—they gave me a schnauzer??"

* * *

Q: Why did God make farts smell?
A: So deaf people could enjoy them, too.

Q: What do you call it when deaf people write their names on the back of their shirt collars?
A: Clothes captioning.

Q: What did the blind, deaf, mute quadriplegic kid get for his birthday?
A: A pinball machine.

Q: What did the blind, deaf, mute quadriplegic kid get for Christmas?
A: Cancer.

* * *

Two brothers were opening presents at Christmas. The younger brother unwrapped a dozen presents while the older brother unwrapped just one. Feeling superior, the younger brother taunted the older one, "Ha ha! I got twelve presents and you only have one!"

The older brother replied, "Ha ha, you have a brain tumor."

* * *

One Halloween, a little boy with a stutter went trick-or-treating dressed like a pirate. At the very first house he visited a man who said, "Aaar, matey! You look like a scurvy dog pirate to me. But tell me, where are your buccaneers?"

The little boy's feelings were instantly hurt. "M-m-m-ister," he stammered, "they're on the sides of my b-b-b-buckin' head."

* * *

A deaf-mute walks into a pharmacy to buy condoms. He has difficulty communicating with the pharmacist, and cannot see any condoms on the shelf. Frustrated, the deaf-mute unzips his pants, places his penis on the counter, and puts a $5 bill next to it.

The pharmacist unzips his pants, and does the same as the deaf-mute. After a moment the pharmacist pockets the money and zips back up. Exasperated, the deaf-mute begins to curse the pharmacist in sign language.

"Look," the pharmacist says, "don't bet if you can't afford to lose."

* * *

Q: What do you get when an epileptic falls into a lettuce patch?
A: Seizure salad.

Q: What do you call an epileptic holding a glass of milk?
A: Milkshake.

Q: What do you throw to an epileptic who's having a fit in the bath?
A: Your laundry.

Q: What do you call an epileptic in a wheelchair?
A: A transformer.

Q: What do you call an epileptic cow?
A: Beef jerky.

* * *

Q: Did you hear about the dyslexic lawyer?
A: He studied all year for the bra exam.

Q: Did you hear about the dyslexic pimp?
A: He bought a warehouse.

Q: Why was the homeless dyslexic man permanently homeless?
A: His sign read, "Will fork for wood."

Q: What do you get when you cross an insomniac, an agnostic, and a dyslexic?
A: Somebody who can't fall asleep while pondering the existence of "Dog."

Q: What did the dyslexic rabbi say?
A: Yo.

Q: What did the dyslexic pirate say?
A: Oh oh oy!

Q: What does "DNA" stand for?
A: The National Dyslexic Association

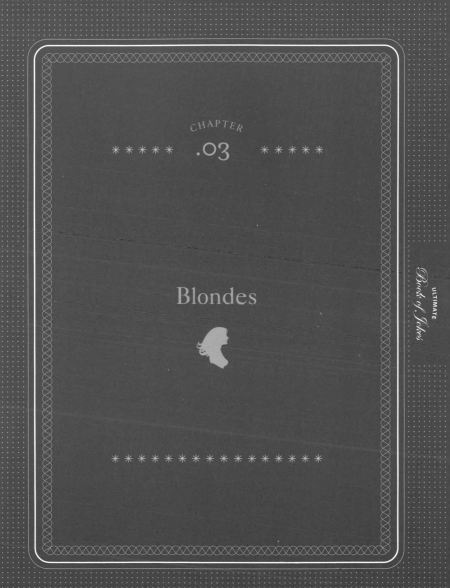

CHAPTER

***** .03 *****

Blondes

* * * * * * * * * * * * * * * * *

CHAPTER 3

Blondes

ARE BLONDES DUMBER THAN EVERYBODY ELSE?

Believe it or not, scientists have investigated this question. Serious people with PhDs have studied the intelligence of blondes versus redheads and brunettes (wouldn't you just love to read the grant proposal?). And the answer from science is—no!

Blondes are neither smarter nor dumber than the rest of humanity. They're equally smart (or equally dumb) depending on how full of water your glass is.

Which begs the question, why do blondes get such a bum rap in the first place? Blame their stereotypical good looks and their often lascivious portrayals in film and mass media. The perverted logic here is that if something looks so damn good, it must be dumb. It's a textbook case of sour grapes from the non-blonde world.

The question of blondes being dumb may be settled. But there's another nagging question about blondes: do they have more fun? If you go by this chapter, the answer is an emphatic yes. Way to go, team!

* * *

Two blondes are walking down the street. One reaches into her purse for a makeup compact and looks into the mirror. "This picture looks like someone I know," she says.

Her blonde friend has a look and says, "Of course, dummy. It's me!"

* * *

A blonde walks into a library and says, "Can I have a burger and fries?"

The librarian says, "I'm sorry, this is a library."

So the blonde whispers, "Can I have a burger and fries?"

* * *

Two blondes were driving through Louisiana when they came to a sign that said "Natchitoches—5 miles." They argued all the way there about how to pronounce the name of the town. Finally they stopped for lunch. After getting their food, one of the blondes said to the cashier, "Can you settle an argument for us? Very slowly, tell us where we are."

The cashier leaned over the counter and said, "Taaaacoooo Beellllll."

* * *

Q: How do you confuse a blonde?
A: You don't. They're born that way.

Q: Why do blondes hate M&M's?
A: They're too hard to peel.

Q: What do you call twenty blondes in a freezer?
A: Frosted Flakes.

Q: What do you call a blonde behind a steering wheel?
A: Airbag.

Q: Why is it good to have a blonde passenger?
A: You get to park in the handicap zone.

Q: What do you do if a blonde throws a grenade at you?
A: Pull the pin and throw it back.

Q: What do you call it when a blonde dyes her hair brunette?
A: Artificial intelligence.

Q: Why did the blonde stare at the can of frozen orange juice?
A: Because it said "Concentrate."

Q: What did the blonde say when she opened the box of Cheerios?
A: "Honey, look at this—doughnut seeds."

Q: Why should blondes never be given coffee breaks?
A: It takes too long to retrain them.

Q: Why did the blonde put lipstick on her forehead?
A: Because she was trying to make up her mind.

Q: What do you call an eternity?
A: Four blondes at a four-way stop.

* * *

A police officer stopped a blonde for speeding and asked nicely to see her driver's license.

She replied in a huff, "Can't you guys get your act together? Just yesterday you take away my license and then today you expect me to show it to you."

* * *

Q: Why does it take longer to build a blonde snowman than a regular one?
A: Because you have to hollow out the head.

Q: How do blonde brain cells die?
A: Alone.

Q: Why don't blondes eat pickles?
A: Because they can't fit their head in the jar.

Q: Why did the blonde tiptoe past the medicine cabinet?
A: She didn't want to wake the sleeping pills.

Q: How do you get a blonde to marry you?
A: Tell her she is pregnant.

Q: What will she ask you?
A: "Is it mine?"

Q: Why did God give blondes 2 percent more brains than horses?
A: Because God didn't want them shitting on the street during parades.

Q: How many blondes does it take to change a lightbulb?
A: Two. One to hold the Diet Coke and one to shout, "Daaaddy!"

Q: Why did the blonde climb over the glass wall?
A: To see what was on the other side.

* * *

A blind man walks into a bar, makes his way to a bar stool, and orders a drink. After sitting there for a while, he yells to the bartender, "Hey, you wanna hear a blonde joke?"

The bar falls absolutely quiet. In a very deep, husky voice the woman next to him says, "Before you tell that joke, sir, I think it's only fair that you should know five things: First, the bartender is a blonde girl with a baseball bat. Second, the bouncer is a blonde girl. Third, I'm a blonde with a black belt in karate. Fourth, the woman sitting next to me is a blonde and a professional boxer. Fifth, the lady to your right is a blonde and a decorated war veteran."

She puts her hand on the blind man's arm and says, "Now think about it seriously, mister. Do you still want to tell that blonde joke?"

The blind man thinks for a second, shakes his head, and mutters, "Naw, not if I'm gonna have to explain it five fucking times."

* * *

Two blondes are headed to New York. Two hours into the flight the pilot gets on the intercom and says, "Sorry folks, we just lost an engine. Don't panic, we have three more engines, it's just gonna take us an hour longer to get there."

A half hour later the pilot gets back on the intercom and says, "Sorry folks, we just lost another engine. It's okay, we have two more engines, it's just gonna take us an extra ninety minutes to get there."

One of the blondes turns to her friend and says, "Dammit! If we lose the two last engines we'll be up here all day."

FUN FACT:
THE SCIENCE OF NATURAL BLONDES

Did you know that, according to a study by the World Health Organization (WHO), natural blondes are likely to be extinct within two hundred years because there are too few people carrying the blonde gene? The last natural blonde is likely to be born in Finland in the 2200s.

Actually, this was a hoax. The WHO never commissioned a study on blondes. And yet in 2002 this fake story was plastered across the world's newspapers. Cynics believe it's all part of a long-established anti-blonde movement. It's just like magazine articles that claim men consider dark-haired women most desirable (not true—preference for hair color varies by culture).

And the latest (true) scientific claim? In a twist, scientists have shown that men score lower on a general intelligence test after being shown pictures of blonde women! In a 2007 study, scientists found that men's mental performance dropped because they believed they were dealing with someone less intelligent.

So are blondes really dumb? Nope. The problem is the men who look at them.

* * *

A blonde and a brunette were watching a story on the six o'clock news, about a man ready to jump off a bridge. The brunette turns to the blonde and says, "I bet you a hundred dollars the man will jump."

The blonde replies, "Okay, you're on."

Sure enough, the man jumps and the blonde gives the brunette $100. The brunette says, "I can't accept this money. I watched the five o'clock news and saw the man jump then."

"No, you have to take it," the blonde says. "I watched the five o'clock news, too. But I didn't think he would do it again."

* * *

Q: What's the mating call of the blonde?
A: "I am sooooo drunk!"

Q: What's the mating call of an ugly blonde?
A: "I said, I am sooooo drunk!"

Q: What's the difference between a group of blondes and a good magician?
A: The magician has a cunning array of stunts.

Q: What's the difference between a blonde and the Panama Canal?
A: The Panama Canal is a busy ditch.

Q: Did you hear about the new blonde paint?
A: It's not real bright, but it's cheap and spreads easy.

Q: What did the blonde's left leg say to her right leg?
A: Between the two of us, we can make a lot of money.

Q: What's the difference between a blonde and the *Titanic*?
A: They know how many men went down on the *Titanic*.

Q: What's a blonde's favorite nursery rhyme?
A: Humpme Dumpme.

Q: Why don't blondes use vibrators?
A: They chip their teeth.

Q: Why is a blonde like a doorknob?
A: Because everyone gets a turn.

Q: What do blondes and computers have in common?
A: You never truly appreciate them until they go down on you.

Q: Why don't blondes talk when having sex?
A: Their mothers taught them not to talk with their mouths full.

Q: What's the difference between a blonde and a bowling ball?
A: You can only fit three fingers in a bowling ball.

Q: What does a blonde say after multiple orgasms?
A: "Way to go, team!"

Q: What's the difference between a blonde and a brick?
A: The brick doesn't follow you home after you have sex with it.

Q: What's a blonde's idea of safe sex?
A: Locking the car door.

Q: Why do blondes always turn on the lights after sex?
A: Eventually, the car door always opens.

Q: Why do blondes have big bellybuttons?
A: From dating blonde men.

Q: What do you call a blonde lesbian?
A: A waste.

Q: What's the difference between a blonde and your toothbrush?
A: You don't let your best friend borrow your toothbrush.

Q: What's the difference between a blonde and your job?
A: Your job still sucks after six months.

* * *

Three women are sitting in a doctor's office waiting for the results of their pregnancy tests. The redhead says, "If I'm pregnant it will be a girl, because I was on the bottom."

The brunette replies, "If I'm pregnant I will have a boy, because I was on top."

The blonde stops, thinks a minute, and says, "Then I'm gonna have puppies!"

* * *

A blonde was driving down the street and saw another blonde attempting to fish from a boat in a field. So the blonde in the car shouted, "You do realize how stupid you're being, right? You're never going to catch anything."

The blonde in the boat shouted back, "What are you talking about? Of course I will!"

The blonde in the car shouted back, "You moron! If I could swim, I'd come out there and punch you!"

* * *

A ventriloquist was on stage at a bar in a small town. He was going through his usual run of dumb blonde jokes when a large blonde in the second row stood up and shouted, "I've heard just about enough of your denigrating blonde jokes! What makes you think you can stereotype blondes that way? What does a person's physical attributes have to do with their worth as a human being?"

The ventriloquist looked on in confused amazement.

"It's jerks like you who keep women like me from being respected," she continued, "and from reaching my full potential as a person because you perpetuate discrimination against not only blondes but women at large. All in the name of a few pathetic jokes."

Flustered, the ventriloquist began to apologize. The blonde interrupted, "You stay out of this, mister. I'm talking to that little shithead on your knee."

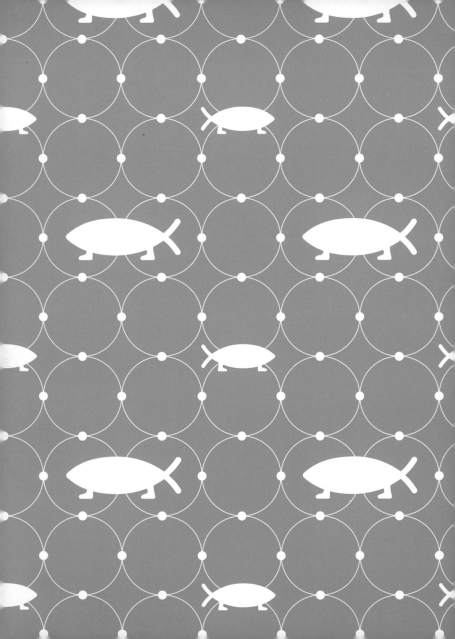

CHAPTER
* * * * * .04 * * * * *

Religion

* * * * * * * * * * * * * * * * *

CHAPTER 4

Religion

THERE'S A CLASSIC JOKE THAT GOES LIKE THIS: A priest, a rabbi, and a mullah walk into a bar together. The bartender looks up and says, "Hey, wait a minute, is this a joke??"

There's something intrinsically funny about religion. While there's no more serious a topic than God in all his/her many forms, things like devils with pointy tails, vestal virgins in Paradise, priestly scandals, and cartoon jihads make religion a ripe topic for poking fun.

On the flip side, you could argue that religious beliefs—no matter how eccentric or extreme—should never be mocked. To this we say, poppy-cock! This chapter is dedicated equally to believers who can take a joke and to people who think organized religion seems rather silly.

If you're priggish or otherwise thin-skinned, please skip this chapter. You may be offended by the content, especially if you believe literally in whatever you're told at your church, temple, mosque, or synagogue.

* * *

A man walks into a confessional and tells the priest, "Father, I'm ninety years old, happily married, and I have five kids. Last night I met two nineteen-year-old girls in a bar and made love to them—both!"

"My son," the priest admonished, "you've committed a grievous sin. When's the last time you were in confession?"

"Father, I've never been to confession before."

"My son, why not?"

"Father, I am Jewish!"

"So why are you telling me this?" the priest asks.

"Why? Are you kidding?? Father, I'm telling everybody!"

* * *

Four Catholic women are having coffee. The first one tells her friends, "My son is a priest. When he walks into a room, everyone calls him 'Father.'"

The second woman chirps in, "My son is a bishop. Whenever he walks into a room, people say, 'Your Grace.'"

The third woman says smugly, "My son is a cardinal. Whenever he walks into a room, people say, 'Your Eminence.'"

The fourth woman sips her coffee and then says, "My son is a gorgeous hard-bodied stripper. When he walks into a room, people say, 'Oh my Lord . . .'"

* * *

Q: How do you make holy water?
A: Fill a pot with water and boil the hell out of it.

Q: How many Christians does it take to screw in a lightbulb?
A: Two, but God only knows how they got in there!

Q: How many conservative Christians does it take to screw in a lightbulb?
A: Five. One to change the bulb and four to testify it was lit from the moment they began screwing.

* * *

I was walking across a bridge and I saw a man standing on the edge, about to jump off. I ran over and said, "Stop! Don't do it!"

"Why shouldn't I?" he asked.

I said, "Well, there's so much to live for."

"Like what?"

"Well, are you religious or atheist?"

"Religious."

"Me too! Are you Christian or Jewish?"

"Christian."

"Me too! Are you Catholic or Protestant?"

"Protestant."

"Me too! Are you Baptist or Episcopalian?"

"Baptist."

FUN FACT:
TOP 5 TASTELESS JESUS JOKES

1) Jesus walks into a hotel, tosses three nails on the front desk, and says, "Hey, can you put me up for the night?"

2) Why did Jesus cross the road?
   Because he was nailed to the chicken.

3) What did Jesus say as he was being crucified?
   Ahhhhhhhhhhh!

4) TAKE 2: What did Jesus say as he was being crucified?
   Don't touch my fuckin' Easter eggs. I'll be back on Monday.

5) Jesus is hanging on the cross, and as his mother is below him, weeping, he looks down and says, "Mother . . ."
   "Yes?" she replies.
   "I can see our house from here."

"Me too! Are you Baptist Church of God or Baptist Church of the Lord in Dominion?"

"Baptist Church of God."

"Me too! Are you Original Baptist Church of God or Reformed Baptist Church of God?"

"Reformed Baptist Church of God."

"Me too! Are you Reformed Baptist Church of God Reformation of 1893 or Reformed Baptist Church of God Reformation of 1917?"

"Reformed Baptist Church of God Reformation of 1917."

To which I said, "Die, heretic scum!" as I pushed him off the bridge.

* * *

A priest is driving along the highway and gets pulled over by the police for speeding. The police officer smells alcohol on the priest's breath and then sees an empty wine bottle on the floor of the car. He asks, "Father, have you been drinking?"

"Just water," says the priest.

The police officer says, "Father, then why do I smell wine?"

The priest looks at the bottle and says, "Good Lord! He's done it again!"

* * *

How many Christians does it take to change a lightbulb?

- ✵ **CHARISMATIC**: Just one. Hands are already up in the air.
- ✵ **ROMAN CATHOLIC**: Zero. Candles are preferred.
- ✵ **PENTECOSTAL**: Ten. One to change the bulb, nine to pray against the Lord of Darkness.
- ✵ **CHRISTIAN SCIENTIST**: Zero, though it takes at least one to sit and pray for the old one to go back on.
- ✵ **CALVINIST**: Zero. God has predestined when the lights will be on.
- ✵ **EPISCOPALIAN**: Ten. One to change the bulb and nine to say how much they like the old one.
- ✵ **MORMON**: Six. One man to change the bulb, five wives to tell him how to do it right.
- ✵ **BAPTIST**: At least twenty. One to change the lightbulb, three committees to approve the change, and one to bake the casserole.
- ✵ **LUTHERAN**: Zero. Sorry, but Lutherans don't believe in change.
- ✵ **ATHEIST**: One. But they are still in darkness.
- ✵ **UNITARIAN**: We choose not to make a statement either in favor of, or against, the need for a lightbulb. However, if in your own journey you have found that lightbulbs work for you, you are encouraged to create a poem or modern dance about your personal relationship with the lightbulb, and present it next Sunday when we will explore a number of lightbulb traditions including incandescent, fluorescent, halogen, compact fluorescent, low-pressure sodium, and LED, all of which are equally valid paths to luminescence.

* * *

Jesus and God are playing golf. They come to a nasty par-4 with trees and water hazards everywhere. Jesus grabs his driver and hits a beautiful shot down the middle of the fairway.

God grabs a 2-iron and shanks one off a tree and into a pond.

All of a sudden there's a blinding flash of light and God's ball appears in the mouth of a fish, which swims to the surface and is speared in the talons of a mighty hawk flying overhead. The hawk flies above the green and the fish drops the ball from its mouth. The ball rolls to the pin and falls into the cup.

Jesus turns to God and says, "You gonna play golf or you gonna fuck around?"

* * *

A man boards a plane and, to his surprise, finds the pope in the seat next to him. Shortly after takeoff, the pope opens the newspaper and starts working on the crossword puzzle. Almost immediately, the pope turns to the man and says, "Excuse me, do you know a four-letter word that ends in 'unt' and refers to a woman?"

Just one word leapt to mind, an extremely vulgar one. The man thinks to himself, "I can't suggest *that* word to the pope. There must be another word . . . "

Then it hits him. He turns to the pope and says, "I think the word you're looking for is 'aunt.'"

"Of course!" exclaims the pope. "I don't suppose you have an eraser?"

* * *

A nun was teaching her young students one day and she asked them what they would like to be when they grew up. A little girl raised her hand and said, "When I grow up I want to be a prostitute."

The nun was shocked and fainted on the spot. When she came around, the nun asked the little girl, "What did you say you wanted to be when you grew up?"

"A prostitute."

"Oh, praise the Lord," the nun replied. "I thought you said a Protestant."

* * *

A guy walks into a bar in a huff and orders a stiff shot of whiskey. Then he asks the bartender, "Hey, how tall's the tallest penguin you've ever seen?"

"Dunno," the bartender says, "about a foot tall. Why?"

"A foot tall--you sure?"

The bartender says, "Yeah, I'm sure. Why?"

"Damn! I just ran over a nun."

* * *

Q: How do you get a nun pregnant?
A: Dress her up as an altar boy.

Q: What is the definition of innocence?
A: A nun working in a condom factory, thinking she's making sleeping bags for mice.

It's easy to make fun of Christians, Jews, and Muslims. You'll get a good laugh out of Buddhists and Mormons, too. Then there are those religions that are so damn weird jokes kinda miss the point. Basically, if your religion *is* a joke, you don't need anybody else piling on *actual* jokes about your wacky beliefs. In that spirit, my five favorite joke religions:

❧ THE UNIVERSE PEOPLE. They live in the Czech Republic and believe that ancient non-earthly beings operate a fleet of spaceships orbiting Earth. The Universe People followers are waiting to be transported into another dimension. Bon voyage, I say.

❧ NUWAUBIANISM. It's a loose term referring to the religion founded by Dwight York, a black supremacist leader and convicted child molester (he's currently in prison serving a 135-year sentence). Some things the Nuwaubianists believe: all humans have seven clones living on different parts of the planet; humans were bred on Mars as part of a *Homo erectus* breeding program gone awry; and famed scientist Nikola Tesla was born on the planet Venus. Amen, brother.

RAJNEESHISM. Bhagwan Shree Rajneesh was an Indian-born mystic who eventually settled in the state of Oregon in the 1980s. The group's claims to religious fame? Preaching that Rolls-Royces were a sign of holiness (Rajhneesh owned dozens of them) and trying to poison nonbelievers by introducing salmonella into salad bars in several Oregon fast-food restaurants.Their god was clearly an angry one.

WORLD CHURCH OF THE CREATOR. It's a white separatist movement advocating a white-only religion called Creativity. Ironically, despite their name, the group does not believe in God. Followers of the World Church of the Creator are—wait for it—atheists!

HEAVEN'S GATE. A cult founded by Marshall Applewhite, whose followers believed that once free of their earthly bodies, a spaceship would take them away to a celestial paradise. The 1997 appearance of the Hale-Bopp comet was a sign their spaceship had arrived. In March of that year, thirty-six members of the cult were found dead in a mass suicide. Their bags were packed. They all wore running shoes and matching uniforms with patches that said "Heaven's Gate Away Team." Each had a $5 bill and a roll of quarters in their pockets. And no, you couldn't make this stuff up if you tried.

Q: What do you call two nuns in a blender?
A: Twisted sisters.

Q: What do you call one nun in a blender?
A: Bloody Mary.

* * *

A priest was confronted by a prostitute. "Do you want a quickie for ten bucks?"

Not knowing what it was, he said no. When he got back to the monastery, his curiosity got the better of him. So he asked a nun, "What's a quickie?"

"Ten bucks, same as in town," the nun answered.

* * *

Four nuns were standing in line at the gates of heaven. St. Peter asked the first if she had ever sinned. "Well, once I looked at a man's penis," she said.

"Put some of this holy water on your eyes and you may enter heaven," St. Peter told her.

St. Peter then asked the second nun if she had ever sinned. "I once held a man's penis," she replied.

"Put your hand in this holy water and you may enter heaven," he said.

Just then the fourth nun pushed ahead of the third nun. St. Peter asked her, "Why did you push ahead in line?"

"Because I want to gargle the holy water before she sits in it!"

* * *

The teacher addressed his class, "I'll give five dollars to anybody who can name the most famous person in the history of the world."

An Irish boy raised his hand up and said, "St. Patrick."

"Sorry Seamus, that's not correct."

Then a French boy raised his hand and said, "Napoleon."

The teacher replied, "I'm sorry, Jean, that's not right either."

Finally, a Jewish boy raised his hand and answered, "It was Jesus Christ."

"That's right, David! You win the five dollars. Congratulations!" As the teacher was handing over the cash he said, "You know David, you being Jewish, I'm surprised you said Jesus Christ."

"Yeah, in my heart I knew it was Moses. But business is business."

* * *

"Oy! I've got good news and bad news about our son," Mrs. Shapiro said to her husband.

"Give me the bad news first!" Mr. Shapiro replied.

"Okay, I just found out our son is a homosexual."

"A homosexual?? What could possible be the good news?"

"He's going with a rich doctor!"

* * *

A Jewish man was hit by a car and knocked down. The paramedics arrived and eased him onto a stretcher in the ambulance. "Are you comfortable?" the paramedic asked.

"I make a good living," the man replied.

* * *

A young boy approached his father at the end of his first day of Hebrew school. "Father, I need five dollars to buy a used textbook for school."

"Four dollars?" the father replied. "What do you need three dollars for?"

* * *

Q: How many Chassidim does it take to change a lightbulb?
A: None. They will never find one that burned as brightly as the first one.

* * *

A Jewish man walks into a bar. After a few drinks he notices a Chinese patron at the end of the bar. The Jewish man walks over and punches him in the face.

"Ouch!" the Chinese man says. "What was that for?"

"That was for Pearl Harbor."

"But I'm Chinese!"

"Chinese, Japanese, what's the difference?" Feeling vindicated, the Jewish patron sits back down.

A minute later the Chinese man walks over to the Jewish man and punches him in the face.

TOP 5 JEWISH MOTHER JOKES

1) Why don't Jewish mothers drink?

   Alcohol interferes with their suffering.

2) What's the difference between a pit bull and a Jewish mother?

   Eventually, the pit bull lets go.

3) What did the waiter ask the group of Jewish mothers?

   Is anything okay?

4) How many Jewish mothers does it take to change a lightbulb?

   No, please don't bother, I'll sit in the dark. I don't want to be a nuisance to anybody.

5) SON: "Hello Mom, how are you?"

   MOM: "Very well, thanks!"

   SON: "Oh, sorry, I must have dialed the wrong number."

"Ouch!" the Jewish man says. "What was that for?"

"That was for the *Titanic*," the Chinese man says.

"But that was an iceberg!"

"Iceberg, Goldberg, what's the difference?"

* * *

A Jewish man was talking to his psychiatrist. "I had a weird dream recently. I saw my mother but then I noticed she had your face. It was so disturbing I couldn't fall back to sleep. I just lay there staring at the ceiling, thinking about it until seven A.M.. I finally got up, made myself a slice of toast and some coffee, and came straight here. Can you please help me explain the meaning of my dream?"

The psychiatrist kept silent for some time and then said, "One slice of toast and coffee? Do you call that a breakfast?"

* * *

A Jewish grandmother walks into a post office to send a package to her son. The postal worker says, "This package is too heavy, you'll need another stamp."

"And that should make it lighter?" the Jewish grandmother asks.

* * *

Q: How does a Jewish kid verbally abuse his playmates?
A: "Your mama pays retail."

Q: What is the difference between a Jewish grandmother and an Italian grandmother?
A: About twenty-five pounds.

Q: What did the Jewish grandmother bank teller say to her customer?
A: "You never write, you never call. You only come to see me when you need money."

Q: What is the most common disease transmitted by Jewish grandmothers?

A: Guilt.

Q: What kind of cigarettes do Jewish grandmothers smoke?

A: Gefiltered.

* * *

A Jewish grandmother is at the beach with her grandson, when a tidal wave sweeps the young boy into the sea. The grandmother immediately falls to her knees and prays to God for the return of her grandson.

"Please God, I have always been a good Jew and a loving bubby. Please, please return my grandson to me."

Just as she finishes her prayer, a big wave comes and washes the boy back onto the beach, good as new. She looks up to heaven and cries, "He had a hat, too!"

* * *

A Jewish grandmother is giving directions to her grandson who is coming to visit. "Come to the front door of the building. I am in apartment seven G. With your elbow push the button next to seven G and I will buzz you in. Come inside, the elevator is on the left. With your elbow, open the elevator and get in, and with your elbow, hit seven. When you get out I am on the left. With your elbow, hit my doorbell."

"Bubby, that sounds easy. But why am I hitting all these buttons with my elbow?"

"What, you're coming empty handed?"

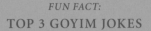

1) Two goyim meet on the street. The first one says, "How's business?"

   The second goy says, "Great. Thanks for asking."

2) A goy walks into a furrier and sees a beautiful fur coat. "What a beautiful coat, my wife will adore it," he says to the clerk. "How much?"

   The clerk replies, "It's on sale for two thousand dollars."

   "Great, I'll take it."

3) A goy calls his mother and says, "Mother, I know I promised to come for dinner tonight, but something has come up and I need to reschedule."

   His mother says. "Okay."

* * *

A Jewish grandmother was watching her two young grandchildren playing in a park. She meets an old friend who says, "What wonderful little boys, these must be your grandchildren. How old are they?"

She replies, "The lawyer is four and the doctor is two."

* * *

A Jewish mother gave her son two shirts for his birthday. The next morning, he came to breakfast wearing one of them.

"I knew it!" she moaned. "You don't like the other one."

* * *

A Jewish grandmother is sitting at the back of a crowded bus packed with passengers. "Oy! I am thirsty. Oy! I am soooooooo thirsty," she complains loudly.

After ten minutes of complaining like this, the passengers on the bus beg the driver to stop the bus so they can get the woman a drink. They pull into a rest stop and get her some water. The bus pulls out and everybody breathes a sigh of relief. Suddenly, from the back of the bus they hear, "Oy, I was thirsty. Oyyyyyyy I was sooooooo thirsty . . . "

* * *

Moses and God are talking one day. God said, "Moses, remember, in the laws of keeping kosher, never cook a calf in its mother's milk. It is cruel."

Moses nods and asks, "Lord, so you are saying we should never eat milk and meat together."

"No," God replies, "what I'm saying is, never cook a calf in its mother's milk."

"Oh Lord, forgive my ignorance!" Moses says. "What you are really saying is we should wait six hours after eating meat to drink milk so the two are not in our stomachs at the same time."

"No, Moses, listen to me," God says. "I am saying, don't cook a calf in its mother's milk."

"Oh, Lord! Please don't strike me down for my stupidity! What you mean is we should have a separate set of dishes for milk and a separate set for meat, and if we make a mistake we have to bury that dish outside."

God shakes his head and says, "Moses, do whatever the hell you like."

* * *

Centuries ago God came down from heaven to earth, went to the Germans, and said, "I have commandments that will help you live better lives."

The Germans asked, "What are commandments?"

The Lord replied, "Rules for living better lives. Here's an example for you: 'Thou shall not kill.'"

"Not kill? We're not interested."

So God went to the Italians and said, "I have commandments . . . "

The Italians wanted an example and the Lord said, "Thou shall not steal."

"Not steal? Not interested."

Next the Lord went to the French saying, "I have commandments . . . "

The French wanted an example and the Lord said, "Thou shall not covet thy neighbor's wife."

The French were not interested.

And then God went to the Jews and said, "I have commandments . . . "

"Commandments," said the Jews, "How much are they?"

"They're free," God replied.

"Free? We'll take ten."

* * *

Q: Why do Jewish men watch porn films backward?
A: They love the bit where the prostitute gives back the money.

Q: What's the technical term for a divorced Jewish woman?
A: Plaintiff.

Q: What's a Jewish woman's idea of natural childbirth?
A: No makeup, whatsoever.

* * *

David is telling a new joke to Isaac. "So Yitzhak and Hymie were talking one day—"

Isaac interrupts him. "What, always with the Jewish jokes! Give it a rest. Why do your jokes always have to be about Jews? Can't you change the names to another ethnic group for once!"

So David starts again, "Matsumoto and Suzuki were talking one day at their nephew's bar mitzvah . . . "

* * *

A priest called the pope with urgent news. "Holy Father, I have good news and bad news. The good news is that Our Lord and Savior, Jesus Christ, has returned to the earth."

"My son, what possibly could be the bad news?" the pope asked.

"Holy Father, I'm calling from Salt Lake City."

* * *

A Jewish man, a Catholic man, and a Mormon man were having drinks at the bar following a business meeting. The Jewish man, bragging about his virility, said, "I have four strong sons. One more and I'll have a basketball team!"

The Catholic man was not impressed. "That's nothing. I have ten sons. One more and I'll have a football team."

To which the Mormon replied, "Gentlemen, I have seventeen wives. One more and I'll have a golf course!"

* * *

Q: What do you get when you cross a kleptomaniac and a Mormon?
A: A basement full of stolen food.

Q: What do you get when you mix LSD and LDS?
A: A high priest.

Q: What's the difference between a virtuous Mormon and a sinful Mormon?
A: The temperature of the caffeine they drink.

Q: Why do you always take two Mormons with you when you go fishing?
A: If you only take one, he'll drink all your beer.

Q: What's great about being a Mormon and living in Tennessee?
A: You can marry *all* your cousins.

Q: Why do Mormon women stop having babies at thirty-five?
A: Because thirty-six is just too damn many.

* * *

A kindergarten teacher gave her class a show-and-tell assignment to bring something to class representing their religion. The first boy stood in front of the class and said, "My name is Daniel. I am Jewish and this is the Star of David."

The second boy stood up and said, "My name is Peter. I am Catholic and this is the Crucifix."

The third boy stood up and said, "My name is Jeremiah. I am Mormon and this is a casserole."

* * *

Q: What goes clip-clop clip-clop clip-clop bang bang?
A: An Amish drive-by shooting.

Q: How can you tell your Amish teenager is in trouble?
A: When you criticize him, he yells, "Thou sucketh!"

Q: TAKE 2: How can you tell your Amish teenager is in trouble?
A: He uses slang expressions like "Talk to the hand, 'cause the beard ain't listening."

* * *

An Amish man and his son went to the city and walked into a tall building. They came upon some doors. An older woman walked up and pressed a button. The doors opened and she went in. The son asked his father what that was for and he said, "I don't know, let's watch what happens."

A few minutes later the doors opened and a beautiful blonde woman walked out. The man turned to his son and said, "Let's go get your mother."

* * *

Q: What did the Buddhist monk say to the hot dog vendor?
A: "Make me one with everything."

Q: What did the hot dog vendor say to the Buddhist monk, when asked if he had change for a five?
A: "Change must come from within."

Q: How many Buddhists does it take to screw in a lightbulb?
A: Four. One to screw it in. One not to screw it in. One both to screw it in and not to screw it in. And one neither to screw it in nor not screw it in.

Q: Why don't Buddhists vacuum in the corners?
A: Because they have no attachments.

Q: What does a Buddhist wish you on your birthday?
A: Many happy returns.

Q: What do you call a schizophrenic Buddhist?
A: Somebody who is at two with the universe.

Q: Why did the Buddhist spill his coffee while driving to work?
A: He had bad kar-mug.

* * *

A man walks into a bar screaming, "All Muslims are shitheads."

A man sitting in the corner shouts, "I take serious offense to that! It's a lie!"

The man asks, "Why? Are you a Muslim?"

"No," he replies, "I'm a shithead."

* * *

A man walks into a sex shop in Jerusalem looking for a sex doll. The clerk asks, "So what kind do you want, Jewish or Muslim?"

The man looks confused and asks, "What's the difference?"

"The Muslim one blows itself up."

* * *

A man is walking down the streets of Belfast late one night when a man jumps out of the shadows holding a machine gun and asks, "Are you Protestant or Catholic?"

The first man responds, "Neither, I'm a Jew."

In a hail of bullets the Jewish man is gunned down. The second man walks away thinking to himself, "I'm the luckiest damn Arab in all of Ireland."

* * *

A Muslim suicide bomber walks into a crowd of infidels and blows himself up. He is immediately transported to Paradise, where he finds himself surrounded by seventy-two of the ugliest women anyone has ever laid eyes upon. The suicide bomber is crestfallen. Allah pats him sympathetically on the shoulder and says, "C'mon, think it through. Why do you think they're still virgins?"

* * *

An Islamic couple, preparing for a religious wedding, meets with their mullah, who asks if they have any final questions. The man asks, "We realize it's a tradition in Islam for men to dance with men, and women to dance with women. But, at our wedding reception, we'd like your permission to dance together."

"Absolutely not," says the mullah. "It's immoral and forbidden in Islam. Men and women always dance separately."

"What about sex?" asks the man.

"Of course!" replies the mullah. "Sex is allowed within marriage."

"What about different positions?" asks the man.

"No problem," says the mullah.

"Woman on top?" the man asks.

"Sure," says the mullah.

"On the kitchen table?" the man asks.

"Yes, of course," says the mullah.

"Can we do it with all of my four wives together watching a porno video?"

"You may, indeed," the mullah says.

"Can we do it standing up?" the man asks.

"No!" says the Mullah.

"Why not?" the man asks.

"Because that could lead to dancing."

* * *

An Arab man is walking through customs at an airport. The customs agent looks at his passport and asks, "Sex?"

"Yes, please!" the Arab man says.

"No, I mean male or female," replies the agent.

"Both. And sometimes camels, too!"

* * *

Q: What's the difference between a Western girl and a Muslim girl?
A: The Western girl gets stoned *before* she commits adultery.

Q: What's the title of Salman Rushdie's latest book?
A: *Buddha You Fat Bastard*.

Q: TAKE 2: What's the title of Salman Rushdie's latest book?
A: *Jesus Was a Lousy Carpenter*.

* * *

Q: What's the biggest problem with being an atheist?
A: Nobody to talk to during an orgasm.

Q: Why did the atheist cross the road?
A: He thought there might be a street on the other side, but he wouldn't believe it until he tested the hypothesis.

Q: What do you get when you cross an atheist with a Jehovah's Witness?
A: Somebody knocking on your door for no apparent reason.

Computers, Math
& Philosophy

****

CHAPTER 5

Computers, Math & Philosophy

ROSES ARE #FF0000, tachyons are gluons not completely dry, and all your base are belong to us.

If you have no idea what I'm talking about, you may not be smart enough (or nerdy enough) to properly enjoy this vigorously intelligent chapter. Perhaps we can interest you in some blonde jokes (please turn to Chapter 3) instead.

* * *

Two atoms are walking down the street and they run into each other. One says to the other, "Are you all right?"

"No, I lost an electron!"

"Are you sure?"

"Yeah, I'm positive."

* * *

Q: What did 0 say to 8?
A: Nice belt!

Q: What did one math book say to the other?
A: Don't bug me. I've got my own damn problems.

Q: Why didn't 4 like 5?
A: Because he was odd.

Q: Why do all the other subatomic particles hate the electrons?
A: Because they're so negative.

Q: Why is 6 scared of 7?
A: Because 7 ate 9 and 10.

* * *

A slightly tipsy mathematician got home at 3 a.m.. His wife was upset and yelled, "You're late! You said you'd be home by 11:45."

The mathematician replied, "No, I am precisely on time. I said I'd be home by a quarter of twelve."

* * *

An infinite number of mathematicians walk into a bar. The first mathematician says, "Bartender, I'll have a beer." The bartender serves him a beer.

The second mathematician says, "I'll have half a beer." The bartender serves him half a beer.

The third mathematician orders ¼ of a beer, the fourth mathematician orders ⅛ of a beer, the fifth mathematician orders 1/16 of a beer, and the sixth mathematician orders 1/32 of a beer when the bartender interrupts and says, "To hell with this, I'll get you fellas two beers."

* * *

Bill Gates died and went to purgatory. God looked down and said, "Well, Bill, I'm really confused on this one. I'm not sure whether to send you to heaven or hell. After all, you helped society enormously by putting a computer in almost every home in the world and yet you created that ghastly Windows 95, Windows ME, Windows Vista, Zune, MSN Music Store, ActiMates—need I go on?? Yet I'm going to do something I've never done before. I'm going to let you decide where to spend eternity."

Bill replied, "Well, thanks, God. So what's the difference between heaven and hell?"

God said, "I'm willing to let you visit both places briefly to help you decide."

Bill said, "Okay, then, let's try hell first." So Bill went to hell.

It was a beautiful, clean, sandy beach with clear waters. There were thousands of beautiful women running around, laughing and frolicking. The sun was shining and the sky was blue. "This is great!" Bill said to God. "If this is hell, I really want to see heaven!"

Heaven was a high place in the clouds, with angels playing harps and singing. It was nice but not as enticing as hell. Bill thought for a quick minute and decided. "I prefer hell."

So Bill Gates went to hell.

Two weeks later, God checked up on Bill in hell. God found him being devoured by demons, burned by eternal flames. "How's everything going, Bill?"

Bill replied, "This is terrible, this is not what I expected. What happened to that other place with the beaches and the beautiful women and the sunny skies?"

God apologized, "Sorry, Bill, that was just the screen saver."

* * *

Q: How many Java programmers does it take to change a lightbulb?
A: One, to generate a "ChangeLightBulb" event to the socket.

Q: How many C++ programmers does it take to change a lightbulb?
A: You're still thinking procedurally. A well-designed lightbulb object would inherit a change method from a generic lightbulb class.

Q: How many Windows programmers does it take to change a lightbulb?
A: Three. One to write WinGetLightBulbHandle, one to write WinQueryStatusLightBulb, and one to write WinGetLight-SwitchHandle.

Q: How many database programmers does it take to change a lightbulb?

A: Three. One to write the lightbulb removal program, one to write the lightbulb insertion program, and one to act as a lightbulb administrator to make sure nobody else tries to change the lightbulb at the same time.

Q: How many software engineers does it take to change a lightbulb?

A: None. That's a hardware problem.

Q: How many Microsoft engineers does it take to change a lightbulb?

A: None. They will redefine darkness as an industry standard.

* * *

A man is puffing on a cigarette. His girlfriend is irritated by the smoke and says, "Can't you read the warning on the cigarette pack? Smoking is terrible for your health."

"You know I am a programmer," he replies. "We don't worry about warnings, we only worry about errors."

* * *

Two mathematicians were eating at a restaurant, arguing about how much math the average person understood. One mathematician claimed most people knew nothing about math. The other claimed most people were surprisingly decent at math.

"Let's make a bet," offered the cynical mathematician. "When I get back from the restroom, we'll ask our waitress a simple math question. If she answers correctly, I'll buy dinner. If not, you buy it." He then excused himself.

The other mathematician called the waitress over. "Listen, when my friend comes back, I'm going to ask you a math question. I don't expect you to understand it, so just answer '169 and 196.'"

FUN FACT:
COMPUTER 1.0

If you spend your days (or nights) on a computer, maybe you, too, yearn for simpler times. Once upon a time mice had tails, monitors were black and white (or green!), and computers were no more complicated than Etch A Sketches.

Q: My Etch A Sketch has funny little lines all over the screen. What do I do?
A: Pick it up and shake it.

Q: How do I turn off my Etch A Sketch?
A: Pick it up and shake it.

Q: What's the shortcut for undo?
A: Pick it up and shake it.

Q: How do I create a new document?
A: Pick it up and shake it.

Q: How do I set the background and foreground to the same color?
A: Pick it up and shake it.

Q: How do I delete a document on my Etch A Sketch?
A: Pick it up and shake it.

Q: How do I save my Etch A Sketch document?
A: Don't shake it.

The first mathematician returned from the bathroom and the second mathematician called the waitress over. "The food was wonderful, thank you so much. By the way, do you happen to know of any three three-digit square numbers that each use the digits 1, 6, and 9 exactly once?"

The waitress looked pensive, scratched her head, bit her thumbnail, and then answered, "Is it 169 and 196?"

Highly annoyed, the cynical mathematician paid the bill. As the waitress walked away she muttered under her breath, "And what about 961?"

* * *

Q: How many constructivist mathematicians does it take to change a lightbulb?
A: None. They do not believe in infinitesimal rotations.

Q: How many topologists does it take to change a lightbulb?
A: Just one. But what will you do with the doughnut?

Q: How many professors does it take to change a lightbulb?
A: One (with eight research students, three programmers, and two postdocs to assist).

Q: How many simulationists does it take to change a lightbulb?
A: Infinity. Each one builds a fully validated model, but the light never actually turns on.

Q: How many graduate students does it take to change a lightbulb?
A: Only one. But it takes eight years.

Q: How many analysts does it take to change a lightbulb?
A: Three. One to prove existence, one to prove uniqueness, and one to derive a nonconstructive algorithm.

Q: How many modal logicians does it take to change a lightbulb?

A: In which world?

Q: How many particle physicists does it take to change a lightbulb?

A: It depends on how excited they are about the job.

Q: How many lightbulbs does it take to change a lightbulb?

A: One, if it knows its Goedel number.

* * *

A physicist, a biologist, and a mathematician were standing across from an empty building. They saw two people enter the building and, an hour later, they saw three people come out.

The physicist said, "That isn't physically possible."

The biologist said, "They must have reproduced."

The mathematician said, "Now there are exactly negative one people in the building."

* * *

Q: A fire is burning in the center of a room. There's a bucket of water in the corner. If an engineer encountered this situation, what would she do?

A: Dump the water in a circle around the fire and let the fire burn itself out.

Q: A fire is burning in the center of a room. There's a bucket of water in the corner. If a physicist encountered this situation, what would she do?

A: Dump the water on the fire and put the fire out.

Q: A fire is burning in the center of a room. There's a bucket of water in the corner. If a mathematician encountered this situation, what would she do?

A: Recognize there was a solution and leave the room.

* * *

Three men are in a hot-air balloon. They find themselves lost in a canyon. One of the men says, "I've got an idea. If we call for help in this canyon, the echo will carry our voices. Hopefully somebody will hear our cries for help."

The men agree it's the best chance they have, so they all shout out together, "Helllloooooo! Where are we?"

Twenty minutes later, they hear an echoing voice say, "Helllloooooo! You're lost!!"

One of the men says, "That must have been a mathematician."

"How do you know that?" one of the other men asks.

"Because he took a long time to answer, he was absolutely correct, and his answer was thoroughly useless."

* * *

Q: An engineer, a physicist, and a mathematician must build a fence around a flock of sheep, using as little material as possible. What does the engineer do?

A: Forms the flock into a circular shape and constructs a fence around it.

Q: An engineer, a physicist, and a mathematician must build a fence around a flock of sheep, using as little material as possible. What does the physicist do?

A: Builds a fence with an infinite diameter and pulls it together until it fits around the flock.

q: An engineer, a physicist, and a mathematician must build a fence around a flock of sheep, using as little material as possible. What does the mathematician do?

a: Builds a fence around himself and defines himself as being outside.

* * *

Two strings walk into a bar and the bartender asks, "So what'll you have?"

The first string says, "I'll have a beer istream& getline(char *buffer, int length, char terminal_char)."

"Please excuse my friend," the second string says. "He isn't null-terminated."

* * *

A SQL statement walks into a bar, sees two tables, and says, "Mind if I join you?"

* * *

q: Why did the chicken cross the Möbius strip?

a: To get to the other . . .

q: Why couldn't the Möbius strip enroll at school?

a: Orientation was required.

q: What is the definition of a tachyon?

a: A gluon that's not completely dry.

q: What is the first derivative of a cow?

a: Prime rib.

q: Did you hear the one about the statistician?

a: Probably.

Q: What happened to the geometer who went to the beach to catch some rays?

A: He came back a tan gent.

Q: What's the difference between a mass spectrometer and an electric guitar?

A: You can tune a mass spectrometer.

Q: What is the longest song in the world?

A: "Aleph-Nought Bottles of Beer on the Wall."

* * *

A man was crossing a road when a frog called out, "If you kiss me, I'll turn into a beautiful princess." He bent over, picked up the frog, and put it in his pocket.

The frog spoke up later and said, "If you kiss me and turn me back into a beautiful princess, I will tell everyone how smart and brave you are and how you are my hero." The man took the frog out of his pocket, smiled at it, and returned it to his pocket.

The frog spoke up again and said, "If you kiss me and turn me back into a princess, I'll stay with you for a year and do anything you want." Again the man took the frog out, smiled at it, and put it back into his pocket.

Finally, the frog asked, "What is the matter? I've told you I'm a beautiful princess, that I'll stay with you for a year and do anything you want. Why won't you kiss me?"

The man said, "Look, I'm a computer programmer. I don't have time for a girlfriend, but a talking frog is cool."

* * *

A famous mathematician was to give a speech at a conference. Asked for a summary, he said he would present a proof of Fermat's Last Theorem—but they should keep it a secret. When he arrived, though, he spoke on a different topic altogether. Afterward the conference organizers asked why he said he'd talk about Fermat's Last Theorem and then didn't.

He replied, "That's my standard practice, just in case I'm killed on the way to the conference."

* * *

Q: How do you get a philosopher off your porch?
A: Pay for the pizza.

Q: What's the difference between a philosopher and an engineer?
A: About $100,000 a year.

Q: What will a philosopher choose: half of an egg or eternal bliss in the afterlife?
A: Half of an egg. Because nothing is better than eternal bliss in the afterlife, and half of an egg is better than nothing.

Q: What's the difference between ignorance and apathy?
A: Don't know, don't care.

* * *

A philosopher went into a closet for ten years to contemplate the question, "What is life?" When he came out, he went into the street and met an old colleague, who asked him where he'd been for the past ten years.

"In a closet," he replied. "I wanted to know what life is really about."

"And have you found an answer?"

"Yes," he replied. "I think it can best be expressed by saying that life is like a bridge."

"That's a wonderful insight, but can you be a little more explicit? Can you tell me how life is like a bridge?"

After some thought the philosopher replied, "Perhaps you are right. Perhaps life is not like a bridge."

* * *

Q: How many philosophers does it take to change a lightbulb?
A: Depends on how you define "change."

Q: How many Hegelians does it take to change a lightbulb?
A: Two. One to argue it isn't dark, one to argue that true light is impossible. This dialectic creates a synthesis, which does the job in the end.

Q: How many Kuhnian constructionist philosophers does it take to change a lightbulb?
A: You're still thinking in terms of incremental change, what's really needed is a paradigm shift, we don't need a bulb with more attributes added on, we need ubiquitous luminescence.

Q: How many existentialists does it take to change a lightbulb?

A: Two. One to change the lightbulb and one to observe how the lightbulb symbolizes an incandescent beacon of subjectivity in a netherworld of cosmic nothingness.

Q: How many fatalists does it take to change a lightbulb?

A: None, why fight it?

Q: How many surrealists does it take to change a lightbulb?

A: Two. One to hold the giraffe and one to fill a bathtub with brightly colored furniture.

* * *

A physicist, a mathematician, and a philosopher were asked to name the greatest invention of all time. The physicist chose fire, which gave humanity power over matter. The mathematician chose the alphabet, which gave humanity power over symbols. The philosopher chose the thermos bottle.

"Why a thermos bottle?" the others asked.

"Because the thermos keeps hot liquids hot and cold liquids cold."

"Yes—but so what?"

"Think about it," said the philosopher. "That little bottle—how does it *know*?"

CHAPTER
***** .o6 *****

Drink, Drank, Drunk

****

CHAPTER 6

Drink, Drank, Drunk

WE OWE THE ROMANS A TREMENDOUS DEBT. Without them there wouldn't be bar jokes. That's because the Romans literally invented the *taberna* (tavern) as a safe haven for weary travelers to rest and to drink. In the eighth and ninth centuries the Anglo-Saxons in Britain took the humble Roman tavern to the next level, creating community-focused ale houses where locals could meet and gossip.

Over the next thousand years the names of these convivial drinking establishments changed from public house to saloon, bar, and cocktail lounge. Yet the characters inside stayed more or less the same. The local drunk, the jaded barfly, the working stiff, the parish priest—these familiar characters have been drinking in the same jokes for years and years.

The classic bar joke follows a rigid format starting with "A man walks into a bar . . ." and ending with a twist. Believe it or not, these jokes have a real-life progenitor: C. B. Palmer. He penned the very first bar joke in a 1952 article for the *New York Times* entitled "The Consummately Dry Martini." Palmer's original bar joke* isn't very funny. But as with the Romans, modern bar humor owes Mr. Palmer a round on the house. A complimentary one, of course. The nuts wouldn't have it any other way.

---

* A man walks into a bar and says he wants a very, very dry martini at a ratio of 25 to 1. The bartender is a little startled but mixes it precisely. As he pours it into just the glass, he asks the customer, "Would you like a twist of lemon with that?" The customer pounds the bar and shouts, "Listen buddy! When I want a goddamn lemonade, I'll ask for one!"

* * *

A grasshopper walks into a bar and the bartender says, "Hey, we have a drink named after you."

The grasshopper says, "What, you have a drink named Murray?"

* * *

A chicken walks into a bar and the bartender says, "I'm sorry, we don't serve poultry."

The chicken says, "That's okay. I just want a drink."

* * *

A bear walks into a bar and says, "I'd like a bourbon and . . . a Coke."

The bartender says, "What's up with the big pause?"

The bear says, "I've had them my whole life."

* * *

A sea anemone walks into a bar and says, "I'd like to buy a beer for that man in the corner."

The bartender brings a beer over to the man and says, "This is from your friend over there."

The man nods and says, "With anemone like that, who needs friends?"

* * *

A horse walks into a bar. The bartender looks up and says, "Hey buddy, why the long face?"

* * *

A horse walks into a bar. The bartender says, "Hey."

The horse says, "Sure."

* * *

A man walks into a bar with a duck on his head. The bartender says, "Can I help you?"

The duck says, "Yeah, can you get this guy off my ass??"

* * *

A duck walks into a bar. The barman says, "Hey, your pants are down."

* * *

A man walks into a bar with a duck on his head. The bartender says, "Hey, where did you get that?"

The duck answers, "Outside. There's thousands of 'em!"

* * *

A woman and a duck walk into a bar. The bartender asks, "Where'd you get the pig?"

"That's not a pig, that's a duck," the woman answers.

The bartender replies, "Look, I was talking to the duck."

* * *

A penguin walks into a bar and orders a drink. The bartender says, "You look like you're wearing a tuxedo."

The penguin says, "What makes you think I'm not?"

* * *

A pony trots into a bar and says, "Bartender, I'd like a beer."

The bartender says, "What? Speak up, I can't hear you."

"A beer," the pony replies, "I'd like a beer."

"What? I still can't hear you," the bartender says. "What's with your voice?"

"Nothing," the pony says. "I'm just a little hoarse."

* * *

A snail slides into a bar and orders a beer. The bartender says, "Sorry, we don't serve snails here," and throws him out.

A few weeks later the snail slides back into the bar and says, "Hey, what did you do that for?"

* * *

A man walks into a bar with a giraffe and they proceed to get loaded. The giraffe drinks so much it passes out on the floor. The man gets up and heads for the door when the bartender yells, "Hey! You can't leave that lyin' there!"

The drunk replies, "That's no lion! It's a giraffe."

* * *

A gorilla walks into a bar and orders a beer. The bartender gives it to him and says, "That'll be fifteen dollars."

The gorilla grumbles under his breath and places a twenty on the counter. The bartender makes change and says, "You know, we don't see many gorillas in these parts."

The gorilla replies, "At these prices I'm not surprised."

* * *

A man walks into a bar with his alligator and asks the bartender, "Do you serve lawyers here?"

"Sure do," the bartender replies.

"Good," says the man. "Give me a beer, and I'll have a lawyer for my gator."

* * *

A man walks into a bar and is surprised to see a horse behind the counter serving drinks. The horse looks up and says, "Hey buddy, what's the problem? You've never seen a horse bartending before?"

"No," the man says, "it's just that I never thought the parrot would sell the place."

* * *

A string walks into a bar with a few friends and orders a beer. The bartender says, "I'm sorry, but we don't serve strings here."

The string walks away and sits down with his friends. A few minutes later he goes back to the bar and orders a beer. The bartender, looking a little exasperated, says, "Like I said, I'm sorry, but we don't serve strings here."

So the string goes back to his table. Then he gets an idea. He ties himself in a loop and messes up the top of his hair. Then he walks back up to the bar and orders a beer. The bartender squints at him and says, "Hey, aren't you a string?"

And the string says, "Nope, I'm a frayed knot."

* * *

A neutron walks into a bar and asks, "How much for a beer?"

The bartender replies, "For you, no charge."

* * *

An E-flat walks into a bar. The bartender looks up and says, "Sorry, we don't serve minors."

* * *

A sans serif font walks into a bar. The bartender says, "Sorry, we don't serve your type here."

* * *

Two jumper cables walk into a bar. The bartender says, "You two better not start anything in here."

* * *

A brain walks into a bar and orders a beer. The bartender looks at him and says, "Sorry, I can't serve you. You're already out of your head."

* * *

A golf club walks into a bar and orders a beer. The bartender looks at him and says, "Sorry, I can't serve you. You'll be driving later."

* * *

An empty beer bottle walks into a bar. The bartender looks up and says, "Hey, weren't you drunk in here last night?"

* * *

A man walks into a bar with a slab of asphalt under his arm and says, "Beer please, and one for the road."

* * *

A three-legged dog walks into an Old West saloon. He slides up to the bar and announces, "I'm looking for the man who shot my paw."

* * *

A man walks into a bar, pulls out a tiny piano and a tiny man. The tiny man starts to play the tiny piano. The bartender asks, "Hey, what's that?"

"It's a twelve-inch pianist. You see, I found this magic lamp, rubbed it, and made a wish. I got a twelve-inch pianist."

"Can I try?" the bartender asks.

"Sure, just rub the magic lamp and make a wish."

A moment later a million ducks fill the room. "Ducks!?" the bartender shouts, "I didn't wish for a million *ducks*. I wished for a million *bucks*."

"What, you think I really wished for a twelve-inch pianist?"

* * *

A man walks into a bar. Half of his head is a giant orange. He orders a beer and the barman says, "I can't help asking: why is half of your head a giant orange?"

"Well," the man replies, "let me tell you all about it. See, a few months ago I got a call from my aunt. She says, 'Hey, I'm cleaning out my attic, do you think you can help? Anything you want, you can have.'

"I'm always happy to help out. So I head on over. A half hour later, covered in dust, I find this antique lamp. It looks good, like the sort of thing you could clean up and sell. So I start rubbing it and—holy crap!—a genie pops out.

"'You have released me from the lamp,' this genie says, 'and I grant you three wishes.'

"Very traditional, but that's okay by me. So I say, 'For my first wish, I want a wallet filled with a million dollars.'

"'Technically that is two wishes,' the genie says, but he's just pulling my leg, he grants my first wish, no problem.

"For my second wish I say—like a total jackass, I'll admit it—'Genie, I want every woman I meet to be desperate to have sex with me.' Fucking stupid, let me tell you. See those women by the door, the ones ogling me, well, it just never ends."

The barman nods, "Amazing, I never thought desperate women could be a problem, but I see your point."

"So anyway," the man continues, "for my third wish I say, 'Genie, I want half of my head to be a giant orange.'"

* * *

A man walks into a bar after a long day at work. As he drinks his beer he hears a quiet voice say, "Wow! You look great!"

The man looks around but can't see where the voice is coming from. A minute later he hears the same soft voice say, "You're so handsome!"

The man looks everywhere but still can't see where the voice is coming from. As he sips his beer he hears the voice again. "What a stud you are!"

The man is baffled and asks the bartender, "What the hell is going on?"

"Don't worry," the bartender says, "it's just the nuts. They're complimentary."

* * *

The next day, the same man walks into the same bar after another long day at work. As he drinks his beer he hears a raspy voice say, "You're a jerk. You look like crap."

The man looks around but can't see where the voice is coming from. A minute later he hears the same raspy voice cough and then say, "I can't stand people like you. You put the 'ugh' in ugly!"

The man asks the bartender, "Hey, what's going on here? Have the complimentary nuts gone rotten?"

"No," the bartender says, "it's the cigarette machine. It's been out of order since we opened."

* * *

Two astronauts walk out of a bar on the moon. "What did you think of that place?" one of the astronauts asked.

"The drinks were okay," the second astronaut replied, "but there was no atmosphere."

FUN FACT:
BEER IS WHAT ALES YOU

Think you like to drink? See how you measure up against the world's foremost drinkers.

When it comes to wine, the world's most prodigious consumers are the Italians (54 liters per person), followed closely by the French (47 liters) and—here's a twist—the Swiss (42 liters). The United Kingdom ties for ninth with the Dutch (both 20 liters), while the United States (7 liters) comes in at a paltry eighteenth on the list.

Wine, sure, that's a sissy's drink. What about beer?

You might think the Irish top the list, since the Emerald Isle boasts no fewer than one pub per 300 inhabitants (women and children included). You'd be wrong. The Irish (131 liters per person) are second after the beer-loving Czechs (157 liters). Cheers, as well, to the Aussies (#4—110 liters), the Brits (#6—99 liters), and the Americans (#14—21 liters).

The *Guinness Book of World Records* honors the town of La Crosse, Wisconsin, for having the most bars per capita (360) and also for having the most bars on one street.

And the record for the most beer consumed in the shortest period of time? The *Guinness Book of World Records* honors Steven Petrosino of Carlisle, Pennsylvania, for quaffing one liter of beer in a mere 1.3 seconds.

* * *

A husband and wife are sitting in their living room. The husband says to his wife, "Honey, I'm going to the pub for a bit, so put your coat on."

The wife asks, "Why, am I going with you?"

"No," the husband replies, "I'm turning off the heat."

* * *

A man walks into a bar, but the bartender tosses him out for being too drunk. The man walks back into the bar a few minutes later, and the bartender tosses him out again for being too drunk. Once again the drunk walks into the same bar. The bartender is just about to toss him out when the man looks at him and asks, "How many bars do you own, anyway?"

* * *

A man is stumbling down the street with one foot on the curb and one foot in the gutter. A cop pulls up and says, "Mister, I've got to take you in. You're clearly drunk."

The man asks, "Officer, are you absolutely sure I'm drunk?"

"Yeah," the cop says, "I'm sure. Let's go."

Obviously relieved, the man says, "Thanks a million, officer. I thought I was a cripple."

* * *

A man walks into a bar and orders a beer. The bartender asks if he wants to buy a raffle ticket. "What's the raffle for?" the man asks.

"It's for a widow with six hungry kids," the bartender replies.

The man shakes his head and says, "Not a chance. I couldn't afford to keep 'em."

* * *

A drunk stumbles out of a bar and runs smack into a passing priest. The drunk looks up and slurs, "Father, pardon me, but I'm Jesus Fucking Christ."

The priest says, "No, my son, you're not."

The drunk says, "Father, I am. I can prove it to you."

So the drunk stumbles back into the bar with the priest in tow. The bartender takes one look at the drunk and says, "Jesus Fucking Christ, you here again?"

* * *

A man walks into a bar and orders a double scotch. After he finishes the drink, he peeks inside his shirt pocket and then asks the bartender for another double scotch. When he finishes that, he again peeks inside his shirt pocket and asks the bartender to bring yet another double scotch. The bartender says, "Look, buddy, I'll pour you drinks all night long. But tell me why you keep looking inside your shirt pocket before ordering a refill."

The man replies, "I'm peeking at a photo of my wife. When she starts looking good, I know it's time to go home."

* * *

A man was drinking heavily at his local bar. By two A.M. he was in no shape to drive, but decided to chance it anyway. A policeman noticed his car speeding and swerving down an otherwise empty road and pulled him over. "Sir, clearly you've been drinking. And what's the hurry—just where do you think you're going?"

"I'm going to a lecture," the man replied.

"And who is going to give a lecture at this hour?" the cop asked.

"My wife."

* * *

A man walks into a bar and notices a woman sitting by herself. He comes in the next day and sees the same woman, sitting alone. After two weeks of seeing her always sitting alone at the bar, he asks her if she'd like to go back to his place and have sex.

"No, thank you," she says politely. "I'm sure this will sound odd in this day and age, but I'm keeping myself pure until I meet the man I love."

"That must be rather difficult," the man suggests.

"Oh, I don't mind too much," she says. "But it has my husband pretty upset."

* * *

A man walks into a bar with his pet monkey. He orders a beer while the monkey starts jumping all over the place. The monkey grabs some olives off the bar and eats them, then grabs some sliced lemons and eats them. Then the monkey jumps on the pool table, grabs the cue ball, sticks it in his mouth, and swallows it whole.

The bartender shouts at the man, "Did you see what your monkey just did?"

The man says, "No, what?"

"He just ate the damn cue ball."

"Yeah, that doesn't surprise me," the man replies. "That monkey eats everything in sight. Don't worry, though, I'll pay for the cue ball and the rest of it." The man finishes his drink, pays his bill, and leaves with the monkey.

A week later the man and the monkey walk back into the bar. The man orders a beer and, just like last time, the monkey starts jumping all over the place. The monkey grabs a maraschino cherry off the bar, sticks it up his butt, pulls it out, and eats it. The bartender is disgusted.

"Did you see what your monkey just did?"

"No, what?" asks the man.

"Your monkey just stuck a maraschino cherry up his butt, then pulled it out and ate it."

"Yeah, that doesn't surprise me," the man says. "He still eats everything in sight, but ever since he ate your damn cue ball he measures everything first."

* * *

Two drunks are kicked out of a bar and start looking for a place to sleep in a dark alleyway. They stumble across a dog curled up comfortably inside a box, licking his private parts. The drunks stand there watching. After a minute one drunk says to the other, "I wish I could do that."

The second drunk looks at him and says, "Well, I think I'd pet him first."

* * *

Three men are drinking in a bar. A drunk stumbles in and then screams at one of the men, "Your mom gives the best blow jobs in town!"

Everyone expects a fight, but the man ignores him and the drunk wanders off.

Ten minutes later the drunk stumbles over and screams at the same man, "I just screwed your mom three times!"

Once again the man refuses to take the bait, and the drunk wanders off.

Ten minutes later, the drunk stumbles back over and shouts, "Your mom even let me—"

The man interrupts and says, "Go home, Dad. You're drunk."

* * *

A man walks into a bar and asks the bartender, "Can I have a pint of less, please?"

"I'm sorry, sir," the bartender replies, looking puzzled. "I've never heard of a drink called less. Is it a beer or a spirit?"

"I have no idea," the man says. "I went to my doctor last week and he told me to drink less."

* * *

A man walks into a bar and asks for ten shots of the bar's finest single-malt whiskey. The bartender sets him up, and the man takes the first shot and pours it on the floor. He then takes the last shot and pours it on the floor.

The bartender asks him, "Why did you do that?"

"Well, the first shot always tastes like crap," the man replies, "and the last one always makes me sick."

* * *

A koala walks into a bar and orders a drink. After a few minutes the koala asks the bartender, "Hey, do you know any place where I can get some action?"

The bartender nods and sends the koala to the back room, where he meets a prostitute. That night the koala has the best sex he's ever had. But when the prostitute asks for money, the koala looks confused.

"I don't mind having sex with a koala," she says. "But time is money, and you gotta pay me."

The koala is flummoxed. "Listen lady, I don't know what sort of koala you think I am, but I don't pay for sex. It's against the rules."

The prostitute asks, "What rules?"

The koala reaches for a dictionary, turns to the letter K, and points to the definition of a koala: "A koala is an animal that eats bush and leaves."

* * *

A man walks into a bar and sees a pretty girl sitting alone at the bar. "Hi, what's your name?" he asks.

"Carmen," she says. "I had my name changed from Stephanie to Carmen because I love cars and I love men. What's your name?"

He thinks for a second and says, "Beersex."

* * *

At the end of a beer conference, the CEOs of three beer companies decided to have a drink together in the hotel bar.

The CEO of Budweiser ordered a Bud, the CEO of Coors ordered a Coors Lite, and the CEO of Miller ordered a Miller Lite. The bartender then asked the CEO of Guinness what he'd like to drink. To everybody's surprise, the CEO of Guinness ordered a Sprite.

"Why don't you order a Guinness?" one of the other CEOs asked.

"Naw. If you guys won't drink beer, then neither will I."

* * *

A man walks into a bar, orders ten shots of bourbon, and starts drinking them down as fast as he can. The bartender asks, "Hey, mister, why are you drinking so fast?"

The man replies, "You would be drinking fast if you had what I had."

"What do you have?" the bartender asks sympathetically.

"About seventy-five cents."

* * *

A man walks into a bar and orders a beer. The bartender serves the drink and says, "That'll be five dollars."

The man opens his wallet and places a $20 bill on the bar. "Sorry, sir," the bartender says, "but I can't accept that."

The man grudgingly pulls out a $10 dollar bill and places it on the bar. The bartender shakes his head and says, "Sorry, sir, but I can't accept that either."

"My money is good. What the hell is going on here?" the man asks.

Pointing to a sign above the door, the bartender explains, "Sir, this is a singles bar."

* * *

A man walks into a bar and orders a beer. As he takes his first sip, a monkey swings down from the rafters, grabs his beer, and runs off. The annoyed man asks, "Who owns that damn monkey?"

The bartender points at the piano player. So the man walks over to the piano player and says, "Do you know your monkey stole my beer?"

"No," the piano player says, "but if you hum it, I'll play it."

* * *

A man walks into a bar and the bartender asks, "What can I get for you?"

"A whiskey on the rocks," the man says.

The bartender pours the drink and says, "That'll be four dollars."

"What are you talking about?" the man asks. "I don't owe you anything for this."

A lawyer sitting nearby and overhearing the conversation says to the bartender, "You know, he's got you there. In the original offer, which constitutes a binding contract, there was no stipulation of remuneration."

The barkeep is not impressed, but says to the man, "Okay, you got me. But don't ever let me catch you in here again."

The next day the same man walks into the bar and the bartender says, "What the hell are you doing in here? I told you never to come back in here!"

"What are you talking about?" the man asks. "I've never been in this bar in my life!"

"I'm very sorry," the bartender says apologetically. "You must have a double."

"Thank you," the man says. "Make it a double whiskey on the rocks."

* * *

A man walks into a bar and orders a triple whiskey. The bartender pours the drink and the man downs it in one gulp. "Excuse me," the bartender says, "I don't mean to pry, but something terrible must have happened to you today."

"Yeah, it did," the man says. "I came home early today, walked up to my bedroom, and found my wife having sex with my best friend."

The bartender pours the man another triple whiskey. "This one's on the house."

The man gulps it down and the bartender asks, "Did you say anything to your wife?"

"Damn straight I did," the man answers. "I told her to pack her bags and get out!"

"What about your friend?" the bartender asks.

"I rolled up a newspaper, looked him straight in the eye, and said, 'Bad dog.'"

* * *

A police officer is waiting outside a bar at closing time, hoping to catch potential drunk drivers. A man stumbles out of the bar, trips on the curb, and tries his keys in half a dozen different cars while the rest of the bar patrons clear out and drive off. Finally, the drunk opens a car door and starts the engine.

The police officer taps on the man's window and says, "Sir, I'm arresting you for drunk driving." The officer administers a breathalyzer test and, to his surprise, gets a reading of 0.00.

The officer says, "I saw you stumble out of the bar and trip over the curb. What's going on here?"

"Surprise!" the driver replies. "Tonight I'm the designated decoy."

* * *

A man walks into a bar and shouts, "Beers for everyone! You, too, bartender!"

But when it's time to pay, the man doesn't have any money. So the bartender roughs him up and tosses him out of the bar.

The next day the same man walks into the same bar and shouts, "Beers for everyone! But not for you, bartender."

"Why not?" the bartender asks.

"Because," the man replies, "you get violent when you drink."

* * *

A man, his son, and a dog walk into a bar.

"Ouch!"

"Ouch!"

"Woof!"

* * *

So a dyslexic walks into a bra . . .

Hippies, Stoners, Rednecks & Bubbas

* * * * * * * * * * * * * * * * *

Hippies, Stoners, Rednecks & Bubbas

IF THIS CHAPTER HAD A THEME SONG, an obvious choice would be Musical Youth's 1982 hit, "Pass the Dutchie." (C'mon, sing along: " . . . I say pass the dutchie on the left hand side . . . pass the dutchie on the left hand side . . . ") The jokes in the first half of this chapter pay homage to drugs, to drug culture, and to those too spaced out to protest being the butt of the joke.

When it comes to rednecks and bubbas, a better theme song would be a tune by Patty Loveless or Tim McGraw, or to most any song plucked from a country music station on the AM dial. Rednecks and bubbas are not mythical creatures—for Americans living in the South, these characters live and breathe. Everybody knows a redneck, and everybody has a bubba in the family. Even so, if you end most sentences with "y'all" and studied the Bible in high school history class, apologies in advance for the second half of this chapter.

* * *

Q: Why do hippies wave their arms when they dance?
A: To keep the music out of their eyes.

Q: How do you know a hippie has been staying at your house?
A: He's still there.

Q: What did the hippie say after the drugs wore off?
A: "Man, this music sucks."

Q: What kind of cigarettes do hippies smoke?
A: Yours.

Q: What's the first thing a Deadhead says at work?
A: "You want fries with that?"

Q: How many hippies can fit in a VW bus?
A: One more, plus a dog.

Q: What's the difference between a hippie and a Deadhead?
A: A hippie gives you the shirt off his back. A Deadhead sells you somebody else's shirt for $15, two for $25.

* * *

A stoner walks into a bar and sees a sign that reads: "Cheese sandwich $2.50, turkey sandwich $3.50, hand job $15."

The stoner checks his wallet and signals to one of the three attractive servers standing behind the bar.

"Can I help you?" she asks, with a knowing smile.

The stoner asks, "Are you the one who gives hand jobs?"

"Yeah," she says sheepishly, "I'm the one."

"Well, go wash your damn hands," the stoner shouts. "I want a cheese sandwich."

* * *

Q: Why is the roach clip called a roach clip?
A: Because "pot holder" was taken.

Q: What do you call it when a roach ash burns your shirt?
A: A pothole.

Q: What do you get when you eat marijuana?
A: A potbelly.

Q: What do you call a stoned epileptic?
A: Shake and baker.

Q: How do you get a one-armed hippie out of a tree?
A: Pass the joint.

Q: If two stoners are in the back of a car, who is driving?
A: The cop.

Q: What do you call a hippie with a haircut?
A: The defendant.

* * *

A stoner called the fire department and said, "Help! Come quick, dude! My house is on fire!"

The fireman replied, "Don't panic, we'll be right over. How do we get there?"

The stoner was dumbstruck. "Dude?! Come in the big red truck."

* * *

Q: How many stoners does it take to change a lightbulb?
A: "Oh wow, is it dark, man?"

Q: How many hippies does it take to screw in a lightbulb?

A: Hippies don't screw in lightbulbs, they screw in sleeping bags.

Q: How many Deadheads does it take to change a lightbulb?

A: They don't change it, they just watch it burn out then follow it around for twenty-five years.

Q: How many Deadheads does it take to change a lightbulb?

A: More than 10,000. One to change the lightbulb; 200 to tape the changing; 1,000 to dance and twirl in ecstasy; 500 to sit and grumble, "They used to change 'em better in the old days"; 100 scalpers selling fake bulbs; 200 local, county, state, and federal officers harassing all the bulb sellers; and the rest to follow the old burned-out bulb to the next gig.

* * *

Q: What happened to the stoner who snorted curry powder by accident?

A: He went into a korma.

Q: Why did the stoner cross the road?

A: His dealer lived on the other side.

Q: Why did the stoner cross the road?

A: He saw people on the other side, standing in a circle and coughing.

Q: Why did the hippie cross the road?

A: Who else would follow a chicken around?

Q: How do you tell if a hippie chick is on the rag?

A: She's only wearing one sock.

Q: What do you call a hippie who just broke up with his girlfriend?

A: Homeless.

Q: What's the difference between an onion and a hippie?
A: Nobody cries when you cut a hippie.

Q: How do you make a stoner's car more aerodynamic?
A: Remove the pizza-delivery sign from the roof.

Q: How do you say "fuck you" in hippie-speak?
A: "Dude, can I borrow your flashlight?"

* * *

Q: How many rednecks does it take to change a lightbulb?
A: Three. One to hold the bulb and two to turn the ladder.

Q: What do a redneck divorce and a tornado have in common?
A: No matter what, somebody's losing a trailer.

Q: How can you tell the toothbrush was invented by rednecks?
A: Because it's not called a teethbrush.

Q: What's the difference between a good ol' boy and a redneck?
A: The good ol' boy raises livestock. The redneck gets emotionally involved.

Q: How do you circumcise a redneck?
A: Kick his sister in the jaw.

* * *

A redneck took his daughter to the gynecologist. The doctor asked, "So what are you here for today?"

The father answered, "To get my daughter on birth control."

"Is your daughter sexually active?" the doctor asked.

"No sir," answered the redneck. "She just lies there like her mother."

* * *

Bubba and his girlfriend fell in love and got married. On their wedding night the new bride says to her husband, "Be gentle with me. I'm a virgin."

Bubba was outraged! He stormed out and swore he'd never again speak to his new wife. Bubba drove straight to his daddy's house to tell him what had just happened. "Daddy, she said she's still a virgin. Can you believe it!!"

Bubba's daddy replied, "Well son, as I've always told you, if she ain't good enough for her own family, she sure ain't good enough for ours."

* * *

A zookeeper notices one of the female gorillas is in heat. That's a problem, because there are no male apes available for mating. So the zookeeper approaches Bubba, who works as a janitor at the zoo. "Bubba," the zookeeper asks, "would you be willing to have sex with that female gorilla for two hundred dollars?"

Bubba accepts the offer, but on three conditions: "First, I don't want to kiss her. Second, you never tell anybody about this. Third, I'm gonna need a week to come up with the two hundred dollars."

* * *

Q: How can you tell you're a redneck Jedi?
A: You've uttered the phrase, "May the force be with y'all."

Q: How can you tell you're a redneck Jedi?
A: At least one wing of your X-wings is primer-colored.

Q: How can you tell you're a redneck Jedi?
A: You've used a light saber to open a bottle of Bud.

Q: How can you tell you're a redneck Jedi?
A: Your landspeeder is up on blocks in the front yard.

Q: How can you tell you're a redneck Jedi?
A: You think the worst part of spending time on Alderaan is the gosh-damn skeeters.

Q: How can you tell you're a redneck Jedi?
A: You heard Uncle Darth say, "Luke, I am your father and your uncle."

* * *

After a day of hunting in the woods, Billy Bob and Bubba were breathing hard, dragging a large deer back to their truck. Another hunter saw them dragging the deer and said, "Boys, I don't want to be nosy, but it's much easier if you drag the deer in the opposite direction. Then the antlers won't dig into the ground."

Billy Bob and Bubba say, "Thanks, mister!" and decide to give it a try.

A few minutes later Billy Bob says, "You know, Bubba, that guy was right. This is a lot easier."

"True enough," Bubba replies, "though we're getting farther away from the truck."

* * *

Bubba was pleasantly surprised to receive an invitation to Passover from his new Jewish neighbors. Bubba sits down for dinner and is served a first course of soup. The neighbor says to Bubba, "This is soup made with matzoh balls."

Historically speaking, "redneck" refers to poor white farmers in the southern United States. Nowadays, at its worst, "redneck" connotes bigotry and racism. At its best it connotes "good ol' boy" Southern conservatism with a hint of low IQ. Ultimately, being a redneck also depends on where you live and what you drive.

∞ If you're American, a redneck is pretty much anybody living south of the Mason-Dixon Line.

∞ If you live south of the Mason-Dixon Line, then a redneck lives in Arkansas.

∞ If you live in Arkansas, then a redneck lives in a trailer.

∞ If you live in a trailer in Arkansas, then a redneck drives a pickup truck.

∞ If you live in a trailer in Arkansas and drive a pickup truck, then a redneck drives a pickup truck with a NASCAR bumper sticker.

∞ If you live in a trailer in Arkansas and drive a pickup truck with a NASCAR bumper sticker, then a redneck drives around with a dog in the back of the truck.

∞ If you live in a trailer in Arkansas and drive a pickup truck with a NASCAR bumper sticker and a dog in the back of the truck—then damn! It sure feels good to be a redneck.

Bubba is hesitant to taste the soup. The neighbor urges him on: "If you don't like it, you don't have to finish it."

Finally, Bubba agrees to eats one matzoh ball with some soup. "My goodness, this *is* delicious," Bubba says. "But I'm wondering, are there any other parts of the matzoh you can eat?"

* * *

A woman walked up to an old man sitting in a chair on his porch. "I couldn't help but notice how happy you look," she said. "What's your secret for a long, happy life?"

The man replied, "Every day I smoke two packs of unfiltered cigarettes, drink a case of beer, eat as much fried food as I can get my hands on, and never, ever exercise."

"That is truly amazing," she said. "So exactly how old are you?"

He proudly replied, "Twenty-five."

* * *

A woman goes into a restaurant in a rural southern town. She orders fried chicken and starts to eat, but right away she starts choking on a chicken bone.

Two bubbas in the next booth notice she is choking, and they get up to help her. The first Bubba drops his pants and bends over, while the second Bubba starts licking the other's ass.

The woman is horrified, and she pukes all over the place, dislodging the chicken bone from her throat.

The first Bubba pulls up his pants and yells to his friend, "You're right! That Hind-Lick Maneuver works like a charm."

* * *

Bubba was driving down a country road one evening when he saw a cop pulling up on him with his lights on. Bubba pulled over, stepped out of his truck, and asked the cop what was wrong. The cop explained, "You were doing seventy-five down this road, and you know the speed limit is just forty."

Bubba told the cop he was wrong, and asked his wife to tell the cop he wasn't speeding. "Officer, I can't tell you if my husband was speeding or not. I have learned to never talk about his driving when he's been drinking like this."

* * *

A guy walks into a redneck bar and orders a glass of wine. Everyone sitting around the bar looks up, expecting to see some flamboyant Yankee. The bartender eyes him suspiciously and asks, "You ain't from around here, are you?"

"No sir," the guy says, "I'm from North Dakota."

"North Dakota?" the bartender asks. "What the hell you do in North Dakota?"

"I'm a taxidermist," the guy replies.

"A taxidermist, what the hell is that?" the bartender asks.

The guy says nervously, "Um, I mount dead animals."

The bartender smiles and shouts out to the whole bar, "It's okay fellas, he's one of us!"

* * *

A man moves into a new house in the rural South. As he's settling in there's a knock on his door. "Howdy," a man says, "I'm your neighbor. I just stopped by to say welcome and to ask you, do you like to drink beer?"

The man says, "Sure, I like to drink beer."

"That's great," the neighbor replies. "How about dancing, do you like to dance?"

"Sure," the man answers, "I don't mind to dance every now and then."

"That's just great," the neighbor replies. "How about screwing, do you like to screw?"

"Um, sure, I guess so," the man answers.

"Perfect," the neighbor replies. "So how about you come to a dance over at my place where there'll be lots of beer and screwing?"

"Okay, why not," the man says. "Will there be lots of women there?"

"No," the neighbor replies, "just you and me."

* * *

Q: What's the politically correct term for "hillbillies"?
A: Hill-williams.

* * *

Bubba and Jeb are on the front porch having a few beers. "How'd you get that black eye?" Jeb asks.

Bubba replies, "My wife and I were watching *Who Wants to Be a Millionaire* in bed. I turned to her and asked, 'Darlin', do you want to have sex with me?'"

"'No,' she answered. Then I said, 'Is that your final answer?' She didn't even look at me, she just said, 'Yes, it's my final answer.'"

"So I said, 'Then I'd like to phone a friend . . . '"

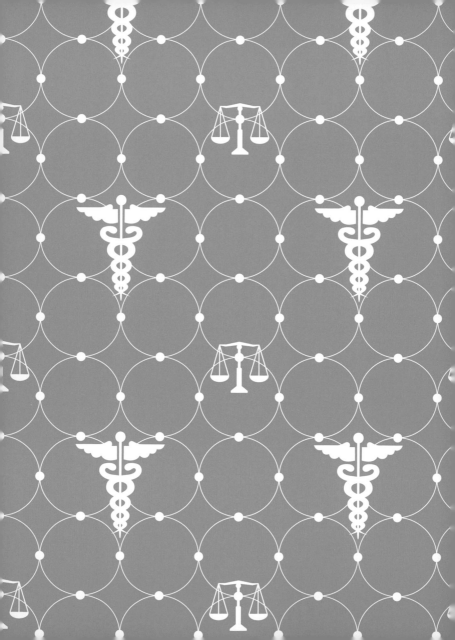

Occupational Hazards

* * * * * * * * * * * * * * * *

CHAPTER 8

Occupational Hazards

YOU KNOW THAT WILLIE NELSON SONG, the one about babies growing up to be doctors and lawyers and such?

Well, Willie, based on this chapter, you couldn't be more wrong. Prospective mamas, encourage your children to be anything except lawyers and doctors. These professions get roughed up, comedically speaking, more than all other professions combined. As career choices go it's safer to be a cannibal. Or an actuary. (The world needs more pirates, too.)

* * *

A fifty-four-year-old accountant left a letter for his wife one evening that read: "My darling wife, I am fifty-four years old and by the time you read this letter I will be at a motel having sex with my beautiful eighteen-year-old secretary."

When he arrived at the hotel, there was a letter waiting for him.

"My darling husband, I am fifty-four years old, as well. By the time you read this letter I will be at a motel with my eighteen-year-old boy toy. Because you are an accountant, you will surely appreciate that eighteen goes into fifty-four many more times than fifty-four goes into eighteen."

* * *

Q: What's the definition of an accountant?
A: Someone who solves a problem you didn't know you had, in a way you won't ever understand.

Q: Why did the accountant cross the road?
A: To bore the people on the other side.

Q: How do you know if an accountant is an extrovert or introvert?
A: An introvert looks at their shoes when talking to you. An extrovert looks at your shoes when talking to you.

Q: Why don't accountants stare out of their office windows during the mornings?
A: Because they'd have nothing to do at lunchtime.

Q: Why did God invent economists?
A: So accountants would have somebody to laugh at.

Q: Why do accountants get excited on Saturdays?
A: They can wear casual clothes to work.

Q: What's an actuary?
A: An accountant without the sense of humor.

Q: How many actuaries does it take to change a lightbulb?
A: None. The insurance department is not allowing any modifications to the bulb at this time.

Q: How many actuaries does it take to change a lightbulb?
A: The same number it took last year, adjusted for trending.

* * *

A man was being audited by the Internal Revenue Service. So he asked his accountant for advice on what to wear. "Wear your shabbiest clothing. Let him think you are dirt-poor," the accountant replied.

Then he asked his lawyer the same question, but got the opposite advice. "Do not let them intimidate you. Wear your best suit and tie."

Confused, the man went to his priest. The priest said, "Let me tell you a story. A woman, about to be married, asked her mother what to wear on her wedding night. 'Wear a heavy, long, flannel nightgown that goes right up to your neck.' But when she asked her best friend, she got conflicting advice. 'Wear your sexiest negligee.'"

The man said, "Father, what does this have to do with my Internal Revenue Service audit?"

"Simple," replied the priest, "it doesn't matter what you wear, you're going to get screwed."

* * *

A patient was visiting her doctor after undergoing a complete physical exam. The doctor said, "I have some very grave news for you. You only have six months to live."

The patient asked, "Oh doctor, what should I do?"

The doctor replied, "Marry an accountant."

"Will that make me live longer?" she asked.

"No," said the doctor, "but it will seem longer."

* * *

Q: What is the definition of an archaeologist?
A: A person whose career is in ruins.

Q: How do you embarrass an archaeologist?
A: Give him a used tampon and ask him which period it came from.

Q. How many archaeologists does it take to change a lightbulb?
A: Are you kidding?! The broken bulb is a national treasure, pointing to our rich history. No, we would rather build a shrine and charge admission to see the "ancient luminosity device."

Q: How many archaeologists does it take to change a lightbulb?
A: 501. One to take the old bulb out, five hundred to proclaim it confirms the biblical record.

* * *

Two cannibals were eating together. The first says, "Man, I hate my mother-in-law."

The second replies, "So try the potatoes."

* * *

Q: For cannibals, what's the hardest part about eating vegetables?
A: The wheelchair.

Q: Why won't cannibals eat divorced women?
A: Too bitter.

Q: What do cannibals do at a wedding?
A: Toast the bride and groom.

Q: What did the cannibal get when he was late for dinner?
A: The cold shoulder.

* * *

Two cannibals capture a clown and drag him back to their village. As they're eating the clown one cannibal asks the other, "Does this taste funny to you?"

* * *

A tourist goes to Africa and asks his guide while walking in the jungle, "Are we safe here? Aren't there cannibals around?"

And the guide says, "Yes, we're safe. There are no cannibals in Africa."

And the tourist asks, "But how can you be sure?"

"Rest assured," the guide says, "we ate the last one on Monday."

* * *

Two cannibals meet in the jungle. The first cannibal says, "You know, I just can't seem to get a tender missionary. I've baked, roasted, stewed, and barbecued them. I've tried every sort of marinade. I just can't seem to get them tender."

The second cannibal asks, "What kind of missionary do you use?"

"The ones that hang out by the river. They wear brown cloaks with a rope around the waist and they're sort of bald on top."

"Ah!" the second cannibal replies. "No wonder, those are friars!"

TOP 10 DOCTOR, DOCTOR! JOKES

1) Doctor, Doctor! I feel like a pack of cards.
   I'll deal with you later.

2) Doctor, Doctor! Can I get a second opinion?
   Of course, come back tomorrow.

3) Doctor, Doctor! I think I'm a bridge.
   What's come over you?

4) Doctor, Doctor! I keep thinking I'm a set of curtains.
   Pull yourself together, man.

5) Doctor, Doctor! You have to help me out.
   Certainly, which way did you come in?

6) Doctor, Doctor! I've broke my arm in two places.
   So don't go back there again.

7) Doctor, Doctor! I feel like a small bucket.
   You do look a little pail.

8) Doctor, Doctor! I feel like a spoon.
   Sit still and don't stir.

9) Doctor, Doctor! I think I'm a wood worm.
   How boring for you.

10) Doctor, Doctor! I've got a strawberry growing out
    of my head.
    I'll give you some cream to put on it.

* * *

A doctor says to her patient, "I've got good news and bad news. Which do you want first?"

The patient says, "Give me the bad news first."

The doctor replies, "Okay, the bad news is, you have brain cancer."

"What?! That's awful news, doc. What about the good news?"

"You've also got Alzheimer's disease," the doctor replies.

The patient looks relieved and says, "Oh, that's not so bad. At least I don't have brain cancer."

* * *

A doctor says to his patient, "I have bad news and worse news."

"Oh dear, what's the bad news?"

"You have only twenty-four hours to live," the doctor answers.

"That's terrible," the patient says. "How can the news possibly get worse?"

"I've been trying to contact you since yesterday."

* * *

A medical student is sent for training at a clinic specializing in sexual disorders. The head of the clinic takes the student on a tour. In the first room they enter, there's a patient masturbating.

"What's his diagnosis?" the student asks.

"He has a severe case of Semen Buildup Disorder. If he doesn't ejaculate multiple times a day, he becomes disoriented and nauseated."

In the second room they find a patient with his pants down around his ankles, receiving oral sex from a beautiful nurse. "What about his diagnosis?" the student asks.

"Same condition. He just has better health insurance."

* * *

A little girl says to her mom, "A boy in my class asked me to play doctor today."

"Oh, no!" the mother replied. "What happened?"

"Nothing. He made me wait forty-five minutes and then double-billed the insurance company."

* * *

A doctor said to his patient, "I've got some very bad news for you. You are dying and you don't have much time left."

"Oh no! That's awful," the man said. "How long do I have?"

"Ten," the doctor replied sadly.

"Ten?!" the man screamed. "Ten what—days, months, weeks?"

The doctor interrupted, "Nine . . . "

* * *

Four doctors are sitting at a bar talking about work. The first doctor says, "I operated on an accountant today. It was so easy. You open them up and everything inside is numbered."

The second surgeon says, "Accountants are okay, but I prefer librarians. Everything inside is in alphabetical order."

The third surgeon says, "Lawyers get my vote. They're heartless, spineless, and gutless. And their head and anus are interchangeable."

The fourth surgeon nods in agreement. "Lawyers are near-perfect patients, sure. But I still prefer engineers. They always understand when you have a few parts left over at the end."

* * *

An eighty-year-old woman tells her doctor, "I need birth control pills."

A bit flustered the doctor asks, "But you're eighty years old. Why on earth do you need birth control pills?"

The woman replies, "They help me sleep better."

"How do birth control pills help you sleep better?"

"I put them in my granddaughter's coffee, I sleep better at night."

* * *

An artist asked the gallery owner if there had been any interest in his paintings currently on display. "I've got good news and bad news," the owner replied. "The good news is that a gentleman inquired about your work and wondered if it would appreciate in value after your death. When I told him it would, he bought all ten of your paintings."

"That's great! What's the bad news?"

The gallery owner replied, "The guy was your doctor."

* * *

A man went to see his doctor. "You need to stop masturbating," the doctor said.

The man asked, "Why?"

The doctor replied, "Because I'm trying to examine you."

* * *

A beautiful woman visits her new doctor, who is overcome with her beauty. All his professionalism goes right out the window. He tells her to take off her pants, she does, and he starts rubbing her thighs.

"Do you know what I'm doing?" asks the doctor.

"Yes, checking for abnormalities," she replies.

He tells her to take off her shirt and bra; she takes them off. The doctor begins rubbing her breasts and asks, "Do you know what I'm doing now?"

She replies, "Yes, checking for cancer."

Finally, he tells her to take off her panties, lays her on the table, gets on top of her, and starts having sex with her. He says to her, "Do you know what I'm doing now?"

"Yes, getting herpes," she replies. "That's why I'm here."

* * *

Q: What did the nurse say when she found a rectal thermometer in her pocket?
A: "Some asshole has my pen."

Q: What's the difference between an oral thermometer and a rectal thermometer?
A: The taste.

Q: What's the difference between a nurse and a nun?
A: A nun only serves one god.

Q: How many doctors does it take to change a lightbulb?
A: Three. One to find a bulb specialist, one to find a bulb-installation specialist, and one to bill Medicare.

* * *

Two nurses overheard a doctor yelling, "Tetanus! Measles! Polio!"

"Why is that doctor yelling?" one nursed asked another nurse.

She replied, "He just likes to call the shots around here."

* * *

A patient goes to his dentist and says, "I have yellow teeth, what do I do?"

The dentist replies, "Wear a brown tie."

* * *

The dentist says to his patient, "I have to pull this tooth, but don't worry, it will take just five minutes."

The patient asks, "And how much will it cost?"

The dentist replies, "A hundred dollars."

"A hundred dollars for just a few minutes' work?" the patient asks.

"I can pull it more slowly if you like."

* * *

A husband and wife enter a dentist's office. The husband says, "I want a tooth pulled. I don't want gas or Novocain because I'm in a terrible hurry. Just pull the tooth as quickly as possible."

"You're a brave man," the dentist says. "Now, show me which tooth it is."

The husband turns to his wife and says, "Open your mouth, dear, and show the dentist which tooth it is."

* * *

A man jumps out of an airplane with a parachute. As he falls, he realizes his parachute is broken. He doesn't know anything about parachutes, but as the earth rapidly approaches, he sees another man shooting up past him.

In desperation, the man with the parachute looks up and yells, "Hey, do you know anything about parachutes?"

The guy flying up looks down and yells, "No, do you know anything about gas stoves?"

* * *

Q: What do you call a pregnant flight attendant?
A: Pilot error.

Q: What's the difference between God and an airline pilot?
A: God doesn't think he's an airline pilot.

Q: How do you know when you're halfway through a date with a pilot?
A: He says, "That's enough about flying, let's talk about me."

Q: How many flight attendants does it take to change a lightbulb?
A: A hundred. One to change it and ninety-nine to bitch about it.

* * *

It's dinnertime on an airplane. The flight attendant asks an economy passenger if he would like dinner. "What are my choices?" he asks.

"Yes or no," she replies.

* * *

A passenger drops his luggage on the scale at an airline counter in Miami and says to the check-in clerk, "I'm flying to New York. I want the duffel bag to go to Denver and the suitcase to go to Los Angeles."

"I'm sorry, sir," the clerk replies, "but we can't do that."

"Why not? You did it last time."

* * *

Two men are drinking at a bar. One man turns to the other and says, "I see that you work for the airlines. Are you a mechanic?"

"Well, no," the second man says. "I operate the equipment that removes human waste from incoming aircraft."

"You must get paid plenty to do a job like that."

"Are you kidding?"

"Well, at least the benefits must be good," the first man says, hopefully.

"Benefits?!" the second man exclaims. "We have to buy our own insurance. Our retirement plan has been canceled. And when I try to fly somewhere on vacation, I always get bumped."

"So why don't you quit?"

"What, and leave aviation?"

* * *

A passenger boarding a plane asks the flight attendant, "Is this my plane?"

"No," the flight attendant says, "it belongs to the airline."

"Don't try to be funny," the passenger replies. "I mean, can I take this plane to Chicago?"

"No sir, I'm afraid it's too heavy."

* * *

A man is flying a hot-air balloon and realizes he is lost. He spots a man on the ground below and shouts, "Can you help me? I don't know where I am."

The man below says, "Yes! I can help. You are in a hot-air balloon, hovering approximately fifty feet above the ground and moving west-by-southwest at approximately 2.2 miles per hour."

"You must be an engineer," says the balloonist.

"I am!" replies the man. "How did you know?"

"Everything you have told me is technically correct, but I have no idea what to make of your information. And the fact is, I am still lost."

The man on the ground yells back, "And you—you must be a manager."

"I am!" replies the balloonist, "but how did you know?"

"Well," says the man, "you don't know where you are or where you are going, and you expect me to solve your problem. The fact is you are in the exact same position you were in before we met, but now it is somehow my fault."

* * *

Q: How many managers does it take to change a lightbulb?
A: None. They prefer to keep their employees in the dark.

* * *

Q: How can you tell when a firefighter is dead?
A: The remote control slips from his hand.

Q: How many firefighters does it take to change a lightbulb?
A: Four. One to change the bulb and three to chop a hole in the roof.

Q: A Mexican fireman had two sons. What did he name them?
A: Hosea and Hoseb.

* * *

A turtle was mugged by a gang of snails on a dark street. A police detective asked the turtle for a description of the assailants. The turtle looked at the detective with a confused look and replied, "I don't know, it all happened so fast."

* * *

Q: What do you call a clairvoyant midget who escapes from police custody?
A: A small medium at large.

Q: How many cops does it take to throw a man down the stairs?
A: None. He fell.

Q: What did the policeman say to his belly button?
A: You're under a vest.

Q: How many cop jokes are there?
A: Just three. All the rest are true.

* * *

A policeman pulls a man over for speeding and asks him to get out of the car. After looking the man over he says, "Sir, I couldn't help but notice your eyes are bloodshot. Have you been drinking?"

The man gets indignant and says, "Officer, I couldn't help but notice your eyes are glazed. Have you been eating donuts?"

* * *

A cop was questioning a young, fit man who had just parked his car in a disabled parking space. The cop asked, "Sir, exactly what is your disability?"

The man replied, "Tourette's. Now fuck off, asshole."

* * *

A policeman stops a woman for speeding and asks to see her license. He looks at it and says, "Lady, it says here that you should be wearing glasses."

"Well, I have contacts," the woman replies.

"I don't care who you know! You're getting a ticket."

* * *

The police arrested two teenagers yesterday. One was drinking battery acid, the other was eating fireworks. The police charged one and let the other one off.

* * *

A police offer sees a woman driving and knitting at the same time. He yells, "Pull over!"

"No officer," she shouts back, "it's a scarf."

* * *

Q: Why won't sharks attack lawyers?
A: Professional courtesy.

Q: What's the definition of mixed emotions?
A: Watching your attorney drive over a cliff in your new car.

Q: How can you tell when a lawyer is lying?
A: Her lips are moving.

Q: What do you have if three lawyers are buried up to their necks in sand?
A: Not enough sand.

Q: How many lawyers does it take to roof a house?
A: Depends how thin you slice 'em.

Q: What happens to lawyers who take Viagra?
A: They get taller.

* * *

A man died and was taken to his place of eternal torment by the Devil. As he passed raging fire pits and shrieking demons, he saw a man he recognized as a lawyer caressing a beautiful woman.

"That's unfair!" he cried. "I have to suffer for all eternity, while the lawyer gets to spend it with a beautiful woman."

"Shut up," screeched the Devil. "Who are you to question that woman's punishment?"

* * *

A fundraiser for a local charity noticed that the town's most successful lawyer hadn't made a donation yet. The fundraiser called the lawyer and said, "Sir, our research shows that out of a yearly income of at least three hundred thousand dollars, you didn't give a dime to charity. Wouldn't you like to give back to the community?"

The lawyer thought it over and replied, "First, did your research also show my mother is dying and has massive medical bills? Or that my sister is confined to a wheelchair? Or that my brother died in a traffic accident, leaving his three children penniless?"

The humiliated fundraiser said simply, "No, sir, I had no idea."

"So if I don't give any money to them," the lawyer said, "why should I give any money to you?"

* * *

Two small boys were talking at the zoo one day. "My daddy's an accountant," the first boy said. "What does your dad do?"

"My daddy's a lawyer," the second boy replied.

"Honest?"

"No, just the regular kind."

* * *

Q: How many lawyers does it take to change a lightbulb?
A: How many can you afford?

Q: How many lawyers does it take to change a lightbulb?
A: Three. One to climb the ladder. One to shake the ladder. And one to sue the ladder company.

Q: How many lawyers does it take to change a lightbulb?
A: You won't find a lawyer who can change a lightbulb. Now, if you're looking for a lawyer to *screw* a lightbulb . . .

TOP 5 DUMBEST LAWSUITS, EVER

Why are lawyers the butts of so many jokes? No doubt the U.S. legal system is partly responsible. When you can sue for whiplash when your exotic dancer's breasts bang your head excessively (true story!), nobody comes out looking good. Especially not the lawyers. Here are five more examples of real-life, honest-to-goodness lawsuits that have been filed in the United States.

❧ LINDSAY LOHAN VS. E*TRADE.
The claim? E*TRADE's Super Bowl ad featured a talking baby named "Lindsay," portrayed as a milk-aholic. Allegedly this ad was subliminally about Lindsay Lohan.

❧ ALLAN HECKARD VS. MICHAEL JORDAN.
The claim? Michael Jordan allegedly looks like him, causing people everywhere to approach him and ask for autographs.

❧ ANNA AYALA VS. THE FAST-FOOD CHAIN WENDY'S.
The claim? She found a finger in her Wendy's chili. The reality? Anna planted the severed finger in her own chili and served four years in prison. She was paroled in 2010 under one condition: never set foot in a Wendy's again.

∾ CLEANTHI PETERS VS. UNIVERSAL STUDIOS.
The claim? The haunted house at Universal's "Halloween Horror Nights" was too scary. Boo!

∾ RICHARD OVERTON VS. ANHEUSER-BUSCH.
The claim? False and misleading advertising. Apparently when Mr. Overton drank a bottle of Budweiser, scantily clad women in bikinis did not magically appear and invite him to play a game of beach volleyball. Case dismissed!

A teacher asked his students what their parents do for a living. One boy stood up and said, "My dad is a piano player in a whorehouse!"

The teacher couldn't believe what he had heard, so he made a point of calling the boy's father to discuss the situation. The boy's father explained, "Actually, I'm a lawyer, but how am I supposed to explain that to a seven-year-old kid?"

* * *

A man phones a law firm and asks, "Can I speak to my lawyer?"

The receptionist says, "I'm sorry, but your lawyer died last week."

The next day the same man phones the law firm and says, "I want to speak to my lawyer."

Once again the receptionist replies, "I'm sorry, but your lawyer died last week."

The next day the man makes his regular call to the law firm and says, "I want to speak to my lawyer."

"Excuse me, sir," the receptionist says, "but this is third time I've had to tell you that your lawyer died last week. Why do you keep calling?"

The man replies, "Because I love hearing you say it!"

* * *

A lawyer is standing in a long line outside a movie theater. Suddenly, he feels a pair of hands massaging his shoulders and neck. The lawyer turns around. "What the hell do you think you're doing?"

"I'm a chiropractor, and I'm just keeping in practice while I'm waiting in line."

"Well, I'm a lawyer, but do you see me screwing the guy in front of me??"

* * *

A man walks into a bar. He sees a good-looking and well-dressed woman sitting on a bar stool. He walks up to her and says, "Hey, beautiful, can I buy you a drink?"

She turns around and says: "Listen, I'll screw anybody, anytime, anywhere, your place, my place, it doesn't matter. I've been doing it ever since I got out of college. I just love to do it."

"No kidding?" he replies, "I'm a lawyer, too! What firm are you with?"

* * *

The pope dies and goes to heaven. When he arrives, St. Peter shows him to his new quarters: a small one-bedroom apartment with no windows. The pope is horrified and demands to know why he's not been given the penthouse suite, considering his many years of service and devotion to the Lord. St. Peter informs him that a lawyer occupies the penthouse suite.

"A lawyer??" exclaims the pope. "But I am the pope! Surely I am more important than a lawyer."

"My apologies, Your Holiness" says St. Peter. "But we have numerous popes here in heaven and just one lawyer."

* * *

Q: What's the definition of an optimist?
A: A folk musician with a mortgage.

Q: What's the least-used sentence in the English language?
A: "Isn't that the banjo player's Ferrari?"

Q: What's the definition of a gentleman?
A: Someone who can play the bagpipes, but doesn't.

Q: What's the difference between a bagpipe player and a terrorist?
A: Terrorists have sympathizers.

Q: Why are harps like elderly parents?
A: Both are unforgiving and hard to get in and out of cars.

Q: What do you call someone who hangs out with a group of musicians?
A: A drummer.

Q: How do you know when there's a drummer at your door?
A: His hat says "Domino's Pizza."

Q: What does a guitar player do when he locks his keys in the car?
A: He breaks the window to get the drummer out.

Q: How can you tell which kid on a playground is the child of a trombonist?
A: He doesn't know how to use the slide and he can't swing.

Q: What's the best thing to play a bodhran with?
A: Two razor blades.

Q: What's a bassoon good for?
A: Kindling for an accordion fire.

1) How do you keep your violin from getting stolen?
   Put it in a viola case.

2) What's the difference between a violin and a viola?
   The viola burns longer.

3) What's the difference between a viola and a coffin?
   The coffin has a dead person on the inside.

4) What's the difference between a viola and a trampoline?
   You take your shoes off to jump on a trampoline.

5) Why do violists have pea-sized brains?
   Because alcohol has swelled them.

* * *

Two musicians are walking down the street. One says to the other, "Who was that piccolo I saw you with last night?"

"That was no piccolo," the other replies, "that was my fife."

* * *

A son says to his mother, "Mom, I want to grow up and be a rock 'n' roll musician."

The mother replies, "That's impossible, son. You have to pick one or the other."

* * *

Q: How many punk rock musicians does it take to change a lightbulb?

A: Two. One to replace the bulb, one to smash the old one on his forehead.

Q: How many drummers does it take to change a lightbulb?

A: None. They have machines that do that now.

Q: How many alto singers does it take to change a lightbulb?

A: None. They can't reach that high.

* * *

A lawyer calls a plumber to fix a leak in his shower. After about thirty minutes the plumber hands him a bill for $300. The lawyer is furious and says, "I'm a lawyer, and even I don't make that kind of money for thirty minutes of work!"

The plumber replies, "Neither did I, when I was a lawyer."

* * *

Q: How many plumbers does it take to screw in a lightbulb?

A: One. One boss to call a plumber, and one plumber to call a helper (who gets his electrician friend to do it on the side).

* * *

A pirate walks into a bar with a ship's steering wheel stuck in his groin. The bartender asks, "What is that steering wheel doing there?"

The pirate replies, "Aaargh! I don't know, but it's driving me nuts."

* * *

Q: What has eight eyes and eight legs?

A: Eight pirates.

Q: How did the pirate stop smoking?
A: He used the patch.

Q: What's a pirate's second-choice job?
A: An aaaarchitect.

Q: Why couldn't the young pirate get into the club?
A: He was caaaarghded.

Q: What's a pirate's favorite kind of socks?
A: Arrrrgyle.

Q: What did Captain Hook die from?
A: Jock itch.

Q: Did you hear about the new pirate movie?
A: It's rated aaaargh.

Q: What's a pirate's favorite style of music?
A: Aaaaargh & B.

* * *

Two psychologists have sex. One turns to the other and says, "That was good for you. How was it for me?"

* * *

A man visits with his psychiatrist wearing only plastic wrap for shorts. The psychiatrist says, "Well, I can clearly see you're nuts."

* * *

A man walks into his psychologist's office and says, "I can't seem to make any friends. Can you help me, you fat ugly bastard?"

* * *

Two psychologists meet at their twenty-fifth college reunion. One of them looks young and energetic, while the other looks old and tired. The older-looking one asks the other, "What's your secret? Listening to other people's problems every day for so many years has made an old man of me."

The other replies, "Who listens?"

* * *

A man walks into his psychologist's office and says, "Doc, my wife thinks I'm crazy because I like sausages."

The psychologist replies, "Nonsense! I like sausages, too."

"Good," the man says. "You should come and see my collection."

* * *

Q: How many psychiatrists does it take to change a lightbulb?
A: None. The lightbulb will change itself, when it's ready.

Q: How many psychiatrists does it take to change a lightbulb?
A: How long have you been having this fantasy?

Q: How many psychiatrists does it take to change a lightbulb?
A: How many do you think it takes?

* * *

Waiter, waiter! This soup tastes funny.
Then why aren't you laughing?

Waiter, waiter! Your thumb is in my soup.
Don't worry, sir, it's not that hot.

Waiter, waiter! There's a twig in my soup.
Hold on, sir, I'll get the branch manager.

Waiter, waiter! I can't eat this chicken, call the manager.
It's no good, sir, he won't eat it either.

Waiter, waiter! Do you have frog legs?
No, sir, I always walk this way.

Waiter, waiter! There is a small slug in this lettuce.
Would you like me to get you a bigger one?

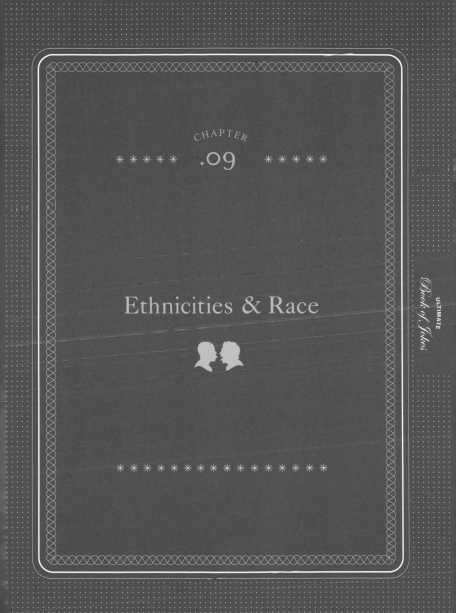

CHAPTER

***** .09 *****

Ethnicities & Race

* * * * * * * * * * * * * * * * *

CHAPTER 9

Ethnicities & Race

RACIST JOKES ARE AN AMERICAN TRADITION. Like it or not, we've always joked about the culture, dress, accents, and cuisine of immigrants. Sometimes the jokes amount to friendly teasing; sometimes it's all about racism and ethnic animosity.

Often racial and ethnic stereotypes are said to "exist for a reason." Is there a sliver of truth in this? Not really. Studies have shown that national and racial stereotypes are not rooted in tangible traits. At some point in the past, perhaps, stereotypes may have contained elements of truth. Yet stereotypes have a hard time keeping up with fast-paced reality. Stereotypes don't evolve. Nations, races, and cultures, on the other hand, constantly evolve.

Racial and ethnic jokes are also the result of historical animosities, when immigrant groups competed for scarce resources, jobs, and social respectability. The United States in the nineteenth and twentieth centuries is full of classic examples. When waves of Chinese came to help build the railroads in the western United States, the so-called chinks were ruthlessly discriminated against. There were also the Irish (there was a time when "No Irish Need Apply" signs were ubiquitous at New York City construction sites), Italians, Poles, Jews, Russians, Mexicans, Vietnamese, Cubans, Arabs; the list goes on and on.

As successive waves of immigrants wash up on America's shores, hungry and tired, mainstream America has always regarded them with animosity and suspicion—and made them the targets of racially charged humor.

* * *

A Chinese couple get married. The new bride is a virgin, and on the wedding night she cowers naked under the sheets as her husband undresses. He climbs in next to her and tries to be reassuring, "My darling, I know this is your first time and you are frightened . . . I promise you, I will do anyting you want. What do you want?"

She smiles coyly and says, "I want number 69."

"Now?? You want beef with broccolli now?"

* * *

Three brothers living in China want to immigrate to the United States. The brothers are named Bu, Chu, and Fu. So they decide to change their names to seem more American. Bu changed his name to Buck. Chu changed his name to Chuck. And Fu got sent back to China.

* * *

Q: Why is there no Disneyland in China?
A: No one's tall enough to go on the rides.

Q: Why can't Chinese barbecue?
A: Because the rice falls through the grill.

Q: What do you call a fat Chinaman?
A: A chunk.

Q: What did the Chinese couple name their special-needs baby?
A: Sum Ting Wong.

* * *

Two Chinese people named Mr. and Mrs. Wong were married and had a child. They asked the doctor if they could see their newborn.

A nurse brought over their baby, but it was a white baby. The two of them said, "Hey, that's not our baby! That's a white baby. We are Chinese and two Wongs definitely don't make a white."

* * *

A Caucasian man was sitting at the bar when a slightly drunk Chinese man said to him, "I am sick of seeing your big round eyes."

The Caucasian replied, "Put on a blindfold."

"Where do I get one?" the Chinese man slurred.

"Here, take my shoelace."

* * *

Q: Why don't Canadians have group sex?
A: Too many thank-you notes to write afterward.

* * *

On the sixth day God turned to the archangel Gabriel and said, "Today I am going to create a land called Canada. It will be a land of natural beauty. It will have majestic mountains and sparkling lakes, forests full of elk and moose, and rivers stocked with salmon."

God continued, "I shall make the land rich in resources to make the inhabitants prosper, I shall call these inhabitants Canadians, and they shall be known as the most friendly people on the earth."

"But Lord," asked Gabriel, "don't you think you are being too generous to the Canadians?"

"Naw," replied God. "Just wait and see the accent I'm going to give them."

* * *

An Englishman, a Canadian, and an American were captured by terrorists. The terrorist leader said, "Before we shoot you, you will be allowed some last words. Please let me know what you wish to talk about."

The Englishman replied, "I wish to speak of loyalty and service to the Queen."

The Canadian replied, "Since you are involved in a question of national purpose, national identity, and secession, I wish to talk about the history of the constitutional process in Canada, special status, distinct society, and uniqueness within diversity."

The American replied, "Just shoot me before the Canadian starts talking."

* * *

Satan was walking through hell one day, making sure things were running smoothly. At the lake of fire he saw a man relaxing in a lawn chair, not sweating or looking uncomfortable at all. Perplexed, Satan approached the man and asked, "Young man, are you not bothered by this heat?"

The man replied, "Not at all. I used to live in downtown Toronto and this weather is just like a typical July day in the city."

Satan didn't like this answer, so he rushed back to the office and turned up the heat in hell another five hundred degrees. Feeling satisfied with himself, Satan again returned to the lake of fire to check on the young man. When he got there, the man was still relaxing in his lawn chair.

Satan asked, "Are you hot and uncomfortable yet?"

The young man looked up and said, "No, the temperature is just like a hot August day in Toronto."

Satan decided to make this man's stay in hell thoroughly unpleasant. He went back to his office, turned the heat off, and turned the air-conditioning on high. The temperature in hell quickly dropped to well below zero and the lake of fire was covered in ice.

Satan walked over to the young man, who was now jumping up and down wildly, waving his arms and yelling madly. "This looks promising!" Satan thought. Coming closer, Satan heard what the man was shouting: "The Maple Leafs have won the Stanley Cup! The Maple Leafs have won the Stanley Cup!"

* * *

Ethan came to work one day, walking with a limp. One of his co-workers noticed the limp and asked, "What happened to you?"

"Oh it's nothing," Ethan said. "I have an old hockey injury that acts up every now and then."

"Gosh Ethan, I never knew you played hockey."

"I don't. I lost five hundred dollars betting on the Maple Leafs and I put my foot through the television."

* * *

Mario Lemieux, Steve Yzerman, and Wayne Gretzky all die and meet in heaven. God is sitting in his Holy Throne and says to Mario, "So Mario, what do you believe in?"

"I believe hockey is the greatest thing in the world and the best sport in the history of mankind," replies Mario.

To which God says, "Fair play, take the seat on my left."

Then God asks Stephen: "So what do you believe in?"

"I believe in courage. To me, it's the quality that best exemplifies Man."

To which God says, "What a keener . . . please take the seat on my right."

Finally God turns to Wayne Gretzky and asks, "What do you believe in?"

Wayne thinks about it for a moment. Then he looks at God and says, "I believe you're sitting in my seat."

* * *

A Canadian man gets drunk and decides to go ice fishing. He grabs his gear and pole, goes out onto the ice, and starts cutting a hole in it. Suddenly he hears a booming voice from above him, "There are no fish there!"

Startled, the man looks around but can't see where the voice is coming from. So he goes back to cutting a hole in the ice. And again the voice booms out, "There are no fish there!"

The Canadian is spooked. He looks up and shouts, "God, is that you?"

"No. This is the skating rink manager."

* * *

Two boys were playing hockey in a park in Toronto. Suddenly one of the boys was attacked by a vicious stray Rottweiler. Thinking quickly, the other boy took his stick, wedged it through the dog's collar, and broke the dog's neck.

A reporter happened to witness the entire incident, and rushed over to interview the boy. "Young Maple Leafs Fan Saves Friend from Vicious Animal," he wrote in his notebook.

"But I'm not a Maple Leafs fan," the boy protested.

"Sorry," the reporter replied, "I just assumed you were. Instead how about 'Young Jays Fan Rescues Friend from Horrific Attack'?"

"I'm not a Jays fan either," the boy said.

The reporter was flummoxed. "I assumed everyone in Toronto was a Maple Leafs or a Jays fan. What team do you root for?"

"I'm a Montreal Canadiens fan," the boy said proudly.

"Okay, so how about 'Little French Bastard from Montreal Kills Beloved Family Pet.'"

* * *

Q: How do you stop a French tank?
A: Say, "Boo."

Q: What is the difference between American fries and French fries?
A: Courage.

Q: After a recent terrorist bombing, what happened to the French terror-alert level?
A: It was raised from "run" to "hide." (The only higher levels are "surrender" and "collaborate.")

Q: How many French soldiers does it take to change a lightbulb?
A: Three. One to roll over, one to surrender to the lightbulb and snitch out occupied sockets, and one to pick up a phone and cry to the United States.

Q: How many Frenchmen does it take to screw in a lightbulb?
A: All of them. One to screw the bulb in, the rest to brag about how great the French are at screwing.

Q: Why do the French smell?
A: So blind people can hate them, too.

Q: What is the difference between a French woman and a basketball team?
A: The basketball team showers after four periods.

Q: Where can you find sixty-two million French jokes?
A: In France.

Q: What's the root of the so-called special relationship between Britain and America?
A: Neither country could be bothered to learn French.

* * *

"Where are you from?" the Englishman asked the American.

"From the greatest damn country in the world!" the American replied.

"Funny," said the Englishman, "you've got the strangest English accent I've ever heard."

* * *

Q: How many Londoners does it take to change a lightbulb?
A: None of your fucking business, mate.

Q: How can you tell you've been in London too long?
A: You can't remember the last time you got up to 30 mph in your car.

Q: How can you tell you've been in London too long?
A: You end every sentence with "mate."

Q: How can you tell you've been in London too long?
A: American tourists no longer annoy you.

* * *

A man rang the bell and a little boy answered the door. "Good morning, young man. Is your father at home?" asked the visitor.

"Nope," replied the boy. "He be out in town."

"Then is your mother around?" the visitor asked.

"Nope, she be goin' with 'im," replied the boy.

"Really, young man," the visitor continued, "your English is atrocious! Where's your grammar?"

"She be in the kitch'un," the boy replied.

* * *

Q: How can you tell you've been in Manchester too long?
A: You think fisherman's hats are attractive.

Q: How can you tell you've been in Manchester too long?
A: You support Man City out of principle.

Q: How can you tell you've been in Manchester too long?
A: You think Londoners are "soft" until they kick your head in at a football match.

Q: How can you tell you've been in Manchester too long?
A: You won't pay more than £2 for a wrap of skag.

* * *

Two East End kids were paddling in the sea at Southend. "Cor," one of the boys said. "Look at your feet. They ain't half dirty."

"Well," the second boy replied, "we didn't have no 'oliday last year."

* * *

Q: How can you tell you've been in Birmingham too long?
A: You have an uncontrollable urge to steal.

Q: How can you tell you've been in Birmingham too long?
A: You often wonder why you don't hear of many Scouse comedians anymore.

Q: How can you tell you've been in Cardiff too long?
A: You're still there.

* * *

An Englishman, a Frenchman, and an Irishman were in a pub talking about their kids. "My son was born on St. George's Day," the Englishman said. "So obviously we decided to call him George."

"What a coincidence," the Frenchman replied. "My daughter was born on Valentine's Day, so we decided to call her Valentine."

"That's bleedin' incredible," the Irishman exclaimed. "Exactly the same thing happened with my son Pancake."

* * *

Q: How can you tell you've been in Dublin too long?
A: You say "I'm grand" all the time.

Q: How can you tell you've been in Dublin too long?
A: You say "Isn't it grand" all the time.

Q: How can you tell you've been in Dublin too long?
A: You say "That'd be grand" all the time.

Q: How can you tell you've been in Dublin too long?
A: You say "Your man" all the time.

Q: How can you tell you've been in Dublin too long?
A: You say "Isn't it grand your man asked if I'm grand" all the time.

* * *

An Englishman, an Irishman, and a Scotsman were drinking together in a pub. The Englishman said, "The pubs in England are the best. You can buy one drink and get a second one free."

The Scotsman replied, "Aye, that's quite good, but in Scotland you can buy one drink and get another two for free!"

"Your pubs sound fine," the Irishman agreed, "but they are not as good as the pubs in Ireland. In Ireland you can buy one pint, get another three for free, and then get taken into the backroom for a shag."

The Englishman and Scotsman both nod and say, "Well, you can't beat that! Did it ever happen to you?"

"No," the Irishman replied, "but it happens to my sister all the time."

* * *

One day two Irishmen are sitting in a pub drinking pints of Guinness. "Excuse me sir," one man says to the other, "but I noticed you look just like me!"

The second man turns around and says, "I noticed the very same thing. Where are you from?"

"I'm from Dublin," says the second man.

"Well, so am I! What street do you live on?"

"Adelaide Road down by the canal," the second man replies.

"Well, so do I! What number are you?"

"Number 39, the red door," the second man replies.

"This is too much of a coincidence, I live at Number 39, too! What are your parents' names?"

"George and Siobhan," the second man replies.

"Absolutely fuckin' unbelievable!" the second man shouts out.

Just then a new customer walks into the pub and asks the bartender, "What's up with them two? They seem a bit overheated."

The bartender replies, "Don't mind 'em. It's just the Murphy twins; they're drunk again."

* * *

Q: What's the difference between an Irish wedding and an Irish wake?
A: One less drunk.

Q: Why did God invent whisky?
A: So the Irish would never rule the world.

Q: Why can't Irishmen ever be lawyers?
A: They can never make it past the bar.

* * *

Two Irishmen, Paul and Patrick, were drifting in a lifeboat after escaping from a sinking ship. While rummaging through the lifeboat's provisions, Patrick found an old lamp. Hoping a genie would appear, he rubbed the lamp vigorously. To his amazement, a genie came forth.

This particular genie, however, said he could offer just one wish, not the standard three. Without giving much thought to the matter, Patrick blurted out, "Turn the entire ocean into Guinness!"

The genie clapped his hands and—poof!—the entire ocean turned into vast sea of Guinness. Paul looked disgustedly at Patrick and, after a long and tense moment, he spoke. "Nice going, Patrick! Now we're going to have to pee in the boat."

* * *

An Irishman went to London and found himself in the Underground late one night. He bought his ticket and was walking to the platform when he saw a sign that read, "Attention: Dogs Must Be Carried on the Escalator."

"For fuck's sake," the Irishman groaned. "Where am I going to find a dog at this hour of the night?"

* * *

An Irishman's wife had been killed in a car accident and the police were questioning him. "Did she say anything before she died?" the officer asked.

"Yes!" the husband replied. "She spoke without interruption for nearly forty years."

* * *

The widow Fitzpatrick came into the newsroom to pay for her husband's obituary. The news editor told her it cost a dollar per word for an obituary, and added, "I remember your husband well. He was a fine man."

The widow thanked him for his kind words and bemoaned the fact she only had three dollars in her purse. Undeterred, she wrote out the obituary: "J. Fitzpatrick died."

The editor said he thought old Fitzpatrick deserved more and he'd give her three more words at no cost. The widow thanked him and rewrote the obituary: "J. Fitzpatrick died. Boat for sale."

* * *

Q: Have you heard about the Irish boomerang?
A: It doesn't come back. It just sings songs about how much it wants to.

Q: How do you confuse an Irishman?
A: Put two shovels against the wall and tell him to take his pick.

Q: How does an Irishman know his wife is dead?
A: The sex is the same, but the dishes start piling up.

Q: Why do Irishmen always carry a little rubbish in their pockets?
A: Identification.

* * *

A young Irish girl goes to confession and says to the priest, "Father, forgive me for I have sinned."

"My child, how have you sinned?" the priest asked.

"Father, I went out with me boyfriend Friday night. We danced, we kissed, and then we made love. Twice!"

The priest said to the young girl, severely, "I want you to go straight home, squeeze six lemons into a glass, and drink it straight down."

"Father, will that wash away my sin?"

"Hardly! But it will get that self-satisfied smile off your face."

* * *

An Irishwoman was in bed with her lover, and had just told him how stupid her husband was when the bedroom door opened. Her husband stood in the doorway, glaring, and shouted, "What are you doing?!"

"There," said the wife, "didn't I tell you he was stupid?"

* * *

An Irishman had no idea his wife was having an affair. So when he came home one day and surprised his wife and lover in the act, he was mad with rage and grief. He grabbed a gun and pointed it at his own head, which made his wife burst out laughing.

"What do you think you're laughing at?" he cried. "You're next."

* * *

A young Scottish boy came home from school and told his mother he had been given a part in the school play. "Wonderful," said the mother, "what part is it?"

"I play the part of the Scottish husband," the boy replied.

The mother scowled and said, "Go back and tell your teacher you want a speaking part."

* * *

Q: Why do Scotsmen wear kilts?
A: So the sheep won't hear the zip.

Q: Why do bagpipers walk when they play?
A: They're trying to get away from the noise.

Q: Why do bagpipers walk when they play?
A: A moving target is harder to hit.

* * *

A Scotsman is walking through a field and sees a man drinking water from a stream with his hand. The Scotsman man shouts, *Awa ye feel hoor thatâs full oâ coos sharn* ("Don't drink the water, it's full of cow shit").

The man shouts back, "I'm English, I speak English, I don't understand you."

The Scotsman shouts back, "Use both hands, you'll get more in."

* * *

A Scotsman, an Englishman, and Julia Roberts were sitting together on a train going through the Scottish countryside. Suddenly the train went through a tunnel and for a moment it was completely dark. There was a kissing noise and the sound of a loud slap. When the train came out of the tunnel, Julia Roberts and the Scotsman were sitting as if nothing had happened. The Englishman was rubbing his face, smarting from a slap to his cheek.

The Englishman was thinking, "The Scottish bloke must have kissed Julia Roberts and she slapped me by accident."

Julia Roberts was thinking, "The Englishman must have tried to kiss me but actually kissed the Scotsman by mistake and got slapped for it."

And the Scotsman was thinking, "This is great. The next time the train goes through a tunnel I'll make a kissing noise and slap that English bastard again."

* * *

Q: How can you tell you've been in Glasgow too long?
A: You say "pish" and "aye" all the time.

Q: How can you tell you've been in Glasgow too long?
A: You end sentences with "like," as in, "Aye, I'm no goin' there, like, it's pish."

Q: How can you tell you've been in Glasgow too long?
A: You have an uncontrollable urge to punch everybody you meet.

Q: How can you tell you've been in Glasgow too long?
A: You punch everybody you meet.

* * *

Angus called his friend's flat, only to find him stripping the wallpaper off the walls. "You're decorating, I see," Angus said.

"No," his friend replied. "I'm moving house."

* * *

Q: Did you hear about the man who was half Irish and half Scottish?
A: He wanted a drink but he couldn't bring himself to buy one.

Q: How many Scotsmen does it take to change a lightbulb?
A: Ach! It's no' that dark.

Q: Did you hear about the two Scotsmen who bet a pint on who could stay under water longer?
A: They both drowned.

Q: Did you hear about the Scotsman who took a beautiful girl for a ride in his taxi?
A: She was so beautiful he could hardly keep his eye on the meter.

Q: What's the definition of a Scottish pessimist?

A: A man who feels badly when he feels good for fear he'll feel worse when he feels better.

* * *

A Scotsman is sitting by himself, looking glum. "I've gone to church every Sunday," he says to himself, "but I'm not known as 'The Christian.' And I've given to charity more than anyone in my town, but I'm not known as 'The Charitable Man.' I've even helped the elderly cross the street, but I'm not known as 'The Helping Hand.' But fuck just one sheep . . . "

* * *

A man walks into a bar with an octopus. He sits the octopus down on a stool and tells everyone in the bar, "This is the world's most talented octopus. He can play any musical instrument you can produce. In fact, I'll wager a hundred dollars that nobody here has an instrument this octopus cannot play."

Somebody in the bar pulls out a guitar. Immediately the octopus picks up the guitar and plays a rip-roaring guitar solo. The man pays up his $100.

Next somebody produces a trumpet. The octopus grabs the horn and plays a sweet melody. The man pays up his $100.

Then a Scotsman pulls out his bagpipes. The octopus fumbles with the pipes and has a confused look.

"Ha!" the Scotsman says. "Ye canny plae it, can ye, octopus?"

The octopus looks up at him and says, "Play it? I'm going to fuck it as soon as I figure out how to remove its plaid pajamas."

An English doctor, being shown around a Scottish hospital, is taken into a ward with a number of patients showing no visible signs of injury. He goes to examine the first man he sees, and the man proclaims, "Fair fa' yer sonsie face, great chieftain e' the puddin' race!"

The Englishman, taken aback, goes to the next patient, who immediately launches into, "Some hae meat, and canna eat, and some wad eat that want it. But we hae meat and we can eat, and sae the Lord be thankit."

The next patient sits up and declaims, "Wee sleekit cow'rin tim'rous beastie, o what a panic's in thy breastie! Thou need na start awa sae hasty, wi' bickering brattle. I wad be laith to run and chase thee, wi' murdering prattle!"

"Well," says the Englishman to his Scottish colleague. "I see you saved the psychiatric ward for last."

"Nay, nay," the Scottish doctor corrects him, "this is the Serious Burns Unit."

* * *

An Aussie, a Kiwi, and a South African walk into a bar and order beers. Quite unexpectedly, the South African finishes his beer, removes his diamond-encrusted watch, pulls out a gun, and shoots the watch to smithereens. He explains, "In South Africa we have so many diamonds we don't need to wear the same diamond twice."

The Kiwi, impressed by this show of bravado, drinks his beer, throws his pint glass into the air, pulls out his own gun, and shoots the pint glass to smithereens. He explains, "Mate, in New Zealand we have so much sand to make glass, we don't need to drink out of the same pint glass twice."

The Australian then pulls out his gun and shoots the Kiwi.

* * *

Q: What's an Australian's idea of foreplay?
A: You awake?

Q: What's a Tasmanian's idea of foreplay?
A: You awake, mum?

Q: What does an Aussie girl use for protection during sex?
A: A bus shelter.

* * *

Three Aussies—Kev, Bruce, and Stevo—are working on a building project. Stevo falls off the roof and is killed instantly. Bruce says, "Somebody should go and tell Stevo's wife."

"Okay," Kev says, "I'm good with girls and that sensitive stuff, I'll do it."

Kev comes back an hour later carrying a slab of beer. Bruce says, "Where did you get that, Kev?"

"Stevo's wife gave it to me," Bruce replies.

"That's unbelievable. You told the lady her husband was dead and she gave you a slab of beer?"

"Not exactly," Kev explains. "When she answered the door I said to her, 'You must be Stevo's widow.'

"She said, 'No, I'm not a widow.'

"And I said, 'I'll bet you a slab of beer you are.'"

* * *

Q: What's the difference between Aussies and pigs?

A: Pigs don't turn into Aussies when they drink.

Q: What's the difference between Aussies and computers?

A: You only have to punch information into a computer once.

Q: How many Aussies does it take to make chocolate chip cookies?

A: Ten. One to make the batter and nine to peel the Smarties.

* * *

An Englishman wanted to marry a French girl but needed to become French first, so the girl's parents would consent. The Englishman went to a doctor who explained, "It is a very simple operation. We simply remove five percent of your brain and you'll wake up French."

The Englishman agreed. After the operation, the doctor rushed into the recovery room with a worried look. "I'm terribly sorry," the doctor said, "there's been a terrible mistake. We accidently removed fifty percent of your brain instead of five percent!"

The Englishman flashed a carefree smile and said, "She'll be right, mate."

* * *

The seven dwarfs went off to work in the mine one day, while Snow White stayed home to make their lunches. When Snow White went to the mine at lunchtime, she found there had been a cave-in. There was no sign of the dwarfs. Tearfully she yelled down the mine entrance, "Is anyone there? Can anyone hear me?"

A faint voice floated up from the bowels of the mine, "Australia will win the Rugby World Cup."

"Thank goodness," said Snow White, "at least Dopey is still alive."

* * *

Q: What do you call fifteen Australians watching the Rugby World Cup final?

A: The Wallabies.

* * *

Two Afghani men were chatting in line, waiting to finalize their Australian residential status. They struck up a friendship and agreed to meet in a year to see who had better adapted to the Australian way of life.

A year later, true to their word, they met. The first man said to the second, "We've integrated completely. Yesterday I ate a meat pie with brown sauce, drank a cold VB, and watched my son play a game of footy with local kids."

The second man replied, "Fuck off, towelhead."

* * *

A Kiwi walks into the local unemployment office and says to the clerk, "I hate being on welfare, I'd really rather have a job."

The clerk says, "Your timing is excellent. We just got a job opening from a very wealthy old man who wants a chauffeur/bodyguard for his nymphomaniac daughter. You'll have to drive around in his Mercedes, but he'll supply all of your clothes. Because of the long hours, meals will be provided. You'll be expected to escort her on international holidays. You'll have a private apartment above the garage. The salary is $100,000 a year."

The Kiwi says, "You're bullshitting me!"

The clerk says, "Yeah, well, you started it."

* * *

Q: Why do New Zealanders love rowing so much?
A: Because they get to sit down and go backward.

* * *

A family of Auckland Blues rugby supporters is out shopping one Saturday. In one of the shops the son picks up a Crusaders rugby jersey and says to his sister, "I've decided to be a Crusaders supporter and I'm buying this jersey."

The sister is outraged and says, "Go talk to mum."

The boy goes off to talk to his mother, Crusaders jersey in hand. "Mum, I've decided to be a Crusaders supporter and I'm buying this jersey."

The mother is outraged and says, "Go talk to your father."

The boy goes off to talk to his father, Crusaders jersey in hand. "Dad, I've decided to be a Crusaders supporter and I'm buying this jersey."

The father is outraged and says, "No son of mine is ever going to be seen in that jersey!"

Later, in the car heading home, the father turns to the son and says, "I hope you've learned an important lesson today."

"Yes, father, I have."

"Good," the dad replies. "What's the lesson?"

"I've only been a Crusaders supporter for an hour," the son says, "and already I hate you Auckland bastards."

* * *

Q: What do you call a Kiwi with a sheep under each arm?
A: A pimp.

Q: How does a Kiwi find a sheep in tall grass?
A: Very satisfying.

Q: What do you call a Kiwi with a goat under one arm and a sheep under the other?
A: Bisexual.

* * *

Two sheepherders, one Aussie and one Kiwi, are flying the herd to a new farm. Suddenly, the plane's engines catch fire and the plane begins to fall quickly to the ground. "Quick!" the Aussies shouts. "Grab a parachute and jump."

"What about the sheep?" the Kiwi shouts back.

"Fuck the sheep," the Aussie says, reaching for a parachute.

The Kiwi thinks for a second and asks, "Do you think we have time?"

* * *

A Kiwi barges into his bedroom carrying a sheep in his arms and says to his wife, "This is the pig I have sex with when you have a headache."

His wife replies, "That's not a pig. It's a sheep, you idiot."

"Shut up," the husband says, "I wasn't talking to you."

* * *

Q: What's the difference between heaven and hell?
A: In heaven the cooks are French, the mechanics are German, the police are English, the lovers are Italian, and everything is organized by the Swiss. In hell the cooks are English, the mechanics are French, the police are Germans, the lovers are Swiss, and everything is organized by the Italians.

Q: What is the traditional Italian version of Christmas?
A: One Mary, one Jesus, thirty-two wise guys.

Q: How can you identify an Italian at a cock fight?
A: He's the one who bets on the duck.

Q: And how can you tell if the Mafia is involved?
A: The duck wins.

Q: How does an Italian get into an honest business?
A: Through the skylight.

Q: What do you call an Italian with his hands in his pocket?
A: Mute.

Q: What do you get when you cross an Italian and a Polak?
A: A guy who makes you an offer you can't understand.

Q: How come Italians don't like Jehovah's Witnesses?
A: They don't like any witnesses.

* * *

An Italian man was bragging to his friends about his sons. "I'ma so prouda my oldest son. He maka eighty thousand dollar evra year. Hesa engineer! I even more prouda ma second son. He maka two hundred thousand dollar a year. Hesa doctor! But, I'ma da proudest a ma youngest son. He maka three million dollar a year. Hesa sports mechanic."

His friend asked, "What's a sports mechanic?"

The dad replied, "Wella, he can fixa everytin. He fixa da horse races, he fixa da boxin match."

* * *

Three men—one French, one English, one Italian—were seated next to each other on an international flight. After a few drinks, the men began discussing their sex lives. "Last night I made love to my wife four times," the Englishman bragged. "And this morning she told me how much she adored me."

"Not bad," the Frenchman says, "though last night I made love to my wife six times. And this morning she told me she could never love another man."

When the Italian remained silent, the Frenchman asked, "And you? How many times did you make love to your wife last night?"

"Once," the Italian man replied.

"Only once?" the Frenchman smugly asked. "And what did she say to you this morning?"

"Don't stop."

* * *

A Greek and an Italian were drinking coffee, arguing over whose culture was superior. The Greek says, "So we have the Parthenon."

"Sure," the Italian replies, "and we have the Colosseum."

"We Greeks gave birth to mathematics."

The Italian nods and says, "Sure, and we built the Roman Empire."

The Greek thinks for a moment and says, "Well, we invented sex."

"That is true," the Italian replies, "but it was the Italians who introduced it to women."

* * *

Q: What's the difference between an Italian grandmother and an elephant?
A: About forty-five pounds and a black dress.

Q: Why do Italians wear gold chains around their necks?
A: So they know where to stop shaving.

Q: Why do Italian men have mustaches?
A: So they can look more like their mammas.

Q: What did the barber say to the Italian kid?
A: "Do you want your hair cut or should I just change the oil?"

Q: Why don't Italians have freckles?
A: They keep sliding off.

* * *

Q: What do you call a pissed-off German?
A: Sauerkraut.

Q: How many Germans does it take to change a lightbulb?
A: One.

Q: What do you get when you cross a Mexican and a German?
A: Beaner-schnitzel.

Q: What did the German kid say when he pushed his brother over a cliff?
A: "Look, mama, no Hans!"

* * *

An American and a German are working together in the same office. The German asks his colleague, "Is it cold in here or is it just me?"

The American replies, "It's just you. You are German, aren't you?"

* * *

A young American couple are unable to have children on their own. So they adopt a German infant and name him Heinrich.

One year goes by and all is well. Two years go by and all is well—apart from the fact that Heinrich has not spoken a single word.

Three, four, five years go by and still Heinrich does not speak. The parents take Heinrich to doctors, speech therapists, psychiatrists, but Heinrich doesn't seem to have any medical or emotional problems. He simply does not speak. By the time Heinrich is eleven, the parents give up trying and accept that Heinrich will never speak.

One day Heinrich is home with his mother, and she makes him soup for lunch. He tastes the soup and—totally unexpectedly—says, "Zee soup iz a little cold, muther."

His mother shouts with joy and smothers Heinrich with kisses. "Sweet Heinrich, why have you never spoken before?"

Heinrich replies, "Until now everyzing has been zatisfaktory."

* * *

Three immigrants—one Italian, one French, one Spanish—are applying for American citizenship. As part of the interview process, they're told they must compose a sentence in English with three primary words: GREEN, PINK, and YELLOW.

The Italian goes the first. "I wake up in the morning. I see the YELLOW sun. I see the GREEN grass. And I think to myself, I hope it will be a PINK day."

The Frenchman is the next. "I wake up in the morning. I eat a YELLOW banana and a GREEN pepper. In the evening I watch PINK Panther on TV."

Finally it's the Spaniard's turn. "I wake up in the morning, I hear the phone GREEN, GREEN, GREEN. Then I PINK up the phone and say YELLOW!"

* * *

An Englishman, a Frenchman, and a North Korean are having a chat. The Englishman says: "I feel happiest when I'm at home, my wool jumper on, sitting in front of a cozy fire."

The Frenchman says: "I feel happiest when I go to a Mediterranean beach with a beautiful woman, and we make love on the sand."

The North Korean says: "In the middle of the night, the secret police knock on the door, shouting, 'Kim Dae-Ho, you're under arrest!' And I say, 'Kim Dae-Ho doesn't live here, he lives next door.' That's when I am happiest!"

* * *

Two North Korean friends are walking down the street. One asks the other, "What do you think of Kim Jong-il?"

"I can't tell you here," the friend replies. "Follow me."

They disappear down a side street. "Now tell me what you think of Kim Jong-il." asks his friend.

"No, not here," says the other, leading him into the hallway of an empty apartment block.

"Okay, tell me here."

"No, not here," the friend replies. "It's still not safe."

They walk down the stairs into the basement of the deserted building. "Okay, now you can tell me what you think of our president."

"Well," says the other, looking around nervously, "I quite like him, actually."

* * *

Two men are talking on a North Korean subway train. "Comrade, by any chance, do you work for the Central Committee?"

"No, I don't."

"Have you worked for the Central Committee before?"

"No, I haven't."

"Are any of your family members working for the Central Committee?"

"No."

"Then please move! You're standing on my foot."

* * *

An Englishman, a Frenchman, and a Russian are in a museum, admiring a painting of Adam and Eve holding an apple in the Garden of Eden. The Englishman says, "The man has something tasty to eat and is eager to share it with the woman. Based on that, I would conclude that they're rather obviously English."

The Frenchman says, "No, I disagree. They're walking around entirely naked, so they must be French."

The Russian says, "There is no doubt they are Russian. They have no clothes to wear, barely anything to eat, and they still think they're in heaven."

* * *

A husband and wife are in bed. The husband turns to his wife and says, "I don't know what's the matter with me. I don't love the Party any more. I feel nothing at all for the Soviet state. What should I do?"

The radio answered, "Please send us your name and address."

* * *

Three prisoners in the old Soviet gulag were comparing notes about why they were there. The first prisoner said, "I'm here because I always got to work five minutes late, and they charged me with sabotage."

The second prisoner nodded and replied, "I am here because I kept getting to work five minutes early, and they charged me with spying."

The third prisoner nodded and replied, "I am here because I got to work on time every day, and they charged me with owning a Western watch."

* * *

Q: Was communism invented by politicians or by scientists?
A: By politicians. Scientists would have tested it on monkeys first.

* * *

Three soldiers—one British, one American, one Russian—are on a joint military exercise. They start talking about how well-fed each of them is. The Russian says, "In the Russian army we have two thousand calories of food a day."

The Englishman says, "In the British army we are given three thousand calories of food a day."

The American says, "In the U.S. army we have four thousand calories of food a day!"

The Russian gets very annoyed and says, "Rubbish! How could one man eat so much cabbage in a day?"

* * *

Near the end of the Cold War, Mikhail Gorbachev received a letter from the Byelorussian Republic requesting approval for a new navy. Gorbachev was annoyed at yet another sign of corruption within the Soviet Union. Gorbachev eventually replied, "You idiot, your Byelorussian Republic is landlocked. What do you need a navy for?"

A week later came the reply. "Uzbekistan has a Ministry of Culture, so why can't we have a navy?"

* * *

A man dies and goes to hell. Satan offers him a choice: he can go to capitalist hell or communist hell. The man asks if he can sample both of them first, before making a decision. Satan agrees and first sends him to capitalist hell. He walks up to somebody being tortured by a demon and asks, "What's it like here?"

"Well," the tortured soul replies, "in capitalist hell they flay you alive, boil you in oil, and then cut you up into little pieces with sharp knives."

"That's terrible! I'm going to check out communist hell."

In a flash the man is waiting in a line outside communist hell. Eventually he gets to the front of the line and asks a demon, "So what's it like in communist hell?"

"Here we flay you alive, boil you in oil, and cut you up into little pieces with sharp knives."

"But that's exactly like capitalist hell!" the man protests. "Why such a long line to get in?"

"Well," sighs the demon, "sometimes we're out of oil, sometimes we don't have knives, sometimes there's no hot water . . ."

* * *

At a United Nations summit the president of the United States said, "I think all countries of the world should unite to end all wars and violence." The assembly applauded.

The president of France said, "I think all countries should unite to end world hunger." The assembly applauded.

The president of Poland stood up and said, "I think . . ." The assembly applauded.

FUN FACT:
CLASSIC POLAK JOKES

Q: How do you sink a Polish battleship?
A: Put it in water.

Q: What happens when a Pole doesn't pay his garbage bill?
A: They stop delivering.

Q: Why is there no ice in Poland?
A: They forgot the recipe.

Q: Why did the Polish submarine sink?
A: Somebody forgot to close the screen door.

Q: Heard about the Polish abortion clinic?
A: There's a twelve-month waiting list.

Q: What does it say on the bottom of Polish Coke bottles?
A: "Open other end."

Q: How many Polaks does it take to change a lightbulb?
A: Three. One to stand on a chair and hold the bulb, plus two to spin the chair.

Q: How do you ruin a Polish party?
A: Flush the punch bowl.

Q: What is long and hard and given to a Polish bride on her wedding night?
A: A new last name.

* * *

A Polish man was suffering from constipation, so his doctor prescribed suppositories. A week later the Pole complained to the doctor that they didn't produce the desired results. "Have you been taking them regularly?" the doctor asked.

"What do you think I've been doing," the Pole replied, "shoving them up my ass?!"

* * *

Lech was an elderly priest in a small Polish town. He had always been a good man and lived by the Bible. One day God decided to reward him. "Lech," the Lord said, "ask me any three questions and I shall answer you."

Lech thought for a moment and then asked, "Will there ever be married Catholic priests?"

God replied, "Not in your lifetime."

Lech then asked, "Will there ever be female Catholic priests?"

God again replied, "Not in your lifetime."

Finally Lech asked, "Will there ever be another Polish pope?"

God replied, "Not in my lifetime."

* * *

A Polish man is hired to paint lines on the highway. On the first day he paints ten miles, and his employer is amazed. On the second day he paints just five miles, and on the third day he paints only one mile of road. Disappointed, his boss asks, "What's the problem? Why are you painting less and less each day?"

The Polish man replies, "Well, every day I have to walk farther and farther to get back to the paint bucket."

* * *

An Englishman is walking down the street when he sees a Polish man with a long pole and a yardstick. The Polish man is standing the pole on its end and trying to reach the top of it with his yardstick.

Sensing the man's ignorance, the Englishman grabs the pole out of his hand, lays it on the ground, and measures it with the yardstick. "There! It's ten feet long."

The Polish man grabs the yardstick and shouts, "You idiot Englishman! I don't care how long it is! I want to know how high it is."

* * *

Three construction workers—one Italian, one Chinese, one Polish—are eating lunch on top of an unfinished building. The Italian is eating a meatball sandwich, the Chinese man has noodles, and the Polish man has knockwurst.

The Italian is tired of eating the same thing every day. "Tomorrow, if I find a meatball sandwich in my lunchbox, I'll throw it off the building!"

The Chinese man agrees. "Tomorrow, if I find noodles in my lunchbox, I will throw them off the building!"

The Polish concurs. "Tomorrow, if I find knockwurst in my lunchbox, I will throw it off the building!"

The next day, sure enough, the Italian and Chinese workers open their lunchboxes and find the usual meatball sandwich and noodles. They both throw their lunches off the building. Without opening it, the Polish man throws his lunchbox off the building too. The other workers ask him how he knew it was knockwurst again without even looking.

The Polish man replied, "Because I pack my own lunch."

First of all, let's get the spelling straight. It's not "Pollock" or "Polok" or "Polack"—it's plain old "Polak," which literally refers to a male Polish person (a female Pole is known as a Polka).

The Polak jokes familiar to most Americans date from the 1950s and '60s, when Polish immigration to the West caused friction with local workers who felt threatened by the influx of cheap unskilled labor from communist Poland.

And that's a point to remember, in case you're offended by the racist tone of these jokes. In many ways the Polaks wandered haplessly into these rude jokes. There's nothing "Polish" in these jokes and very little to illuminate Polish history or culture. Instead, these jokes capture a moment in time when middle-class America felt threatened by yet another wave of poor immigrants competing for scarce jobs.

The good news, for Polaks at least, is that these jokes don't resonate with younger Americans. Kids these days don't remember the Polish influx, and they don't watch old episodes of *All in the Family* (Archie Bunker loved his Polak jokes). And thus the Polak joke begins its slow journey from mainstream to obscure. Do widzenia!

* * *

A Polak, an Englishman, and a German were driving through the desert when their car ran out of gas. They decided to walk for help to the nearest town, which they had passed twenty miles back.

A rancher was sitting on his front porch when he saw the Englishman walk by. The rancher noticed he was carrying a glass of water, so the rancher said, "Hello! Why are you carrying a glass of water through the desert?"

The Englishman explained his predicament and said, "I have a long way to walk, so I brought some water in case I get thirsty."

A while later the rancher noticed the German walking by with a loaf of bread. The rancher said, "Hello! Why are you carrying a loaf of bread through the desert?"

The German explained his predicament and said, "I have a long way to walk, so I brought some food in case I get hungry."

Finally the Polak walked by, dragging a car door. More curious than ever, the rancher said, "Hello! Why are you dragging a car door through the desert?"

The Polak said, "I have a long way to go, so if it gets too hot, I'll roll down the window."

* * *

Yo mama's so fat . . .

- ∽ Her nickname is "Damn!"
- ∽ When you get on top of her your ears pop.
- ∽ She can't even jump to a conclusion.
- ∽ She needs a watch on both arms because she covers two time zones.

- She needs a Hula-hoop to keep her socks up.
- I have to take a bus, a train, and a cab just to get on her good side.
- Her clothes have stretch marks.
- When she goes to a restaurant she doesn't get a menu, she gets an estimate.
- She took a spoon to the Super Bowl.
- She eats Wheat Thicks.
- She sat on four quarters and made a dollar.
- She sat on a rainbow and got Skittles.
- She sat on a scale and it said, "To be continued."
- She was floating in the ocean and Spain claimed her as the New World.

* * *

Yo mama's so ugly . . .

- They filmed *Gorillas in the Mist* in her shower.
- She didn't get hit with the ugly stick, she got hit with the ugly log.
- When she walks down the street people say, "Damn, is it Halloween already?"
- When she entered an ugly contest they said, "Sorry, no professionals."
- Her birth certificate was an apology letter from the condom factory.
- When she was born, the doctor slapped *himself.*
- When she was born her mother said, "What a treasure!" and her daddy said, "Yeah, let's go bury it."

- She looks like her face caught on fire and they put it out with a fork.
- She looks like she's been in a dryer filled with rocks.
- When your dad wants to have sex in the car, he tells her to get out.
- She looks like she got hit with a bag of "What the fuck?!"
- American Express left home without *her*.

* * *

Yo mama's so old . . .

- I told her to act her age, and she died.
- Her beeper number is 1.
- When she was in school there was no history class.
- When God said "Let there be light" she flipped the switch.
- She owes Jesus three bucks.

* * *

Yo mama's so poor . . .

- She got thrown out of a homeless shelter.
- I stepped on a cigarette butt in your house and your mama said, "Who turned off the heat?"
- She's got more furniture on her porch than in her house.
- She wears her McDonald's uniform to church.
- She has to do drive-by shootings on the bus.

* * *

Q: Why do so many white people get lost skiing?
A: It's hard to find them in the snow.

Q: How do you stop five white guys from raping a white woman?
A: Throw them a golf ball.

Q: What does a bird have that white girls don't?
A: Breasts.

Q: What's the flattest surface on the planet?
A: A white girl's ass.

Q: How many white girls does it take to screw in a lightbulb?
A: None. White girls can't screw.

Q: How many white men does it take to screw in a lightbulb?
A: One. White men will screw anything.

Q: What do you call a bunch of white guys sitting on a bench?
A: The National Basketball Association.

Q: What did the black guy do with his M&M's?
A: He ate them.

Q: What did the white guy do with his M&M's?
A: He put them in alphabetical order.

Q: What's twelve inches long, hard, and white?
A: Nothing. It only comes in black.

Q: What does a white man do at the nightclub?
A: Cry while all the colored folk are bumpin' and grindin' with his fine white bitches.

q: What do you say when you see a white man carrying a TV?
a: "Excuse me, sir, you dropped your receipt."

q: What does a white woman make for dinner?
a: Reservations.

q: Why shouldn't white people go swimming?
a: Because crackers get soggy when wet.

✳ ✳ ✳

q: Why did God give black men large penises?
a: As a way of saying "Sorry" for putting pubic hair on their heads.

q: What are the best ten years of a black kid's life?
a: Third grade.

q: What did God say when the second black person was born?
a: Damn. I burnt another one.

q: What's the difference between a black man and a park bench?
a: A park bench can support a family of four.

q: What is the difference between Batman and a black man?
a: Batman can go into a store without robbin'.

q: Why are black people so fast?
a: Because all the slow ones are in jail.

q: How do you get a black kid to stop jumping on the bed?
a: Put Velcro on the ceiling.

q: How do you get him down?
a: Yell "Piñata!" at the Mexican kids next door.

q: Why do you throw a rock at a Mexican on a bike?
a: To get your bike back.

Q: Why do you throw a rock at a black guy on a bike?
A: To get your slave back.

Q: What do black kids get for Christmas?
A: Your bike.

* * *

Q: How many cops does it take to arrest a Mexican?
A: Two. One to arrest him and the other to hold his oranges.

Q: Why don't Mexicans cross the border in groups of three?
A: Because it says "No Trespassing."

Q: What was the last thing Jesus said to the Mexicans?
A: "Don't do anything until I get back!"

Q: Why aren't there any Mexicans on *Star Trek*?
A: They won't work in the future, either.

Q: What do you call two Mexicans playing basketball?
A: Juan on Juan.

Q: What do you call a group of stoned Mexicans?
A: Baked beans.

Q: What do you call a Mexican baptism?
A: Bean dip.

Q: What do you call a midget Mexican?
A: Paragraph. Because he's too short to be an essay.

Q: When does a Mexican become Spanish?
A: When he marries your daughter.

Q: What's a Mexican's favorite bookstore?
A: Borders.

Q: Why can't Mexicans play the game Uno?
A: Because somebody always steals the green cards.

Q: What do you call Mexicans who can't do anything?
A: Mexicants.

Q: How many Mexicans does it take to screw in a lightbulb?
A: Juan.

CHAPTER

***** .10 *****

Turds & Toilets

****

Turds & Toilets

DO YOU THINK FARTS ARE FUNNY? Does diarrhea make you laugh? If you're the kind of person who thinks poop is funny forward, backward, and upside down (did you know poop spells "boob" upside down? Hilarious!), then this chapter is for you.

For some, bathroom jokes are gross and border on shameful. The rest of us see the humor in this great equalizer. It's a fact that Madonna poops and the Queen of England farts. So get over your embarrassment and laugh. It's not taboo, it's just poo!

Go ahead, pull my finger.

* * *

Q: What's the biggest problem working in a paperless office?
A: Needing to shit.

Q: What's eight inches long and starts with a P?
A: A turd.

* * *

Q: What's brown and sits on a piano bench?
A: Beethoven's First Movement.

Q: What's in the toilet of the Starship *Enterprise*?
A: The captain's log.

Q: What do Eskimos get from sitting on the ice too long?
A: Polaroids.

Q: What's the definition of surprise?
A: A fart with a lump in it.

Q: What's the definition of bravery?
A: A man with diarrhea, chancing a fart.

Q: Why don't they have any toilet paper in KFC?
A: Because it's finger-licking good!

Q: What's the definition of a wet fart?
A: A turd honking for the right of way.

* * *

A man was at his doctor's office, complaining. "Doc, I've got really bad gas. I fart all the time. Even more troubling—my farts do not stink and they make no sound. We've been here for five minutes and I've farted a dozen times. And as I said, you couldn't hear or smell them, right?"

The doctor takes a few steps back and says, "Here's a prescription I want you to fill."

"Doc, this is wonderful! This prescription, will it really clear up my farting problem?"

"No. The prescription is to clear up your sinuses. Next week I want you back for a hearing test."

* * *

A woman walks into a shop that sells expensive Persian rugs. Looking around, she spots the perfect rug, walks over, and inspects it. As she bends to feel the texture of the rug she farts loudly.

Rather embarrassed, she looks around to see if anyone has noticed. Standing next to her is a salesman. "Good day, madam, how may I help you?"

Very uncomfortably she asks, "How much does this rug cost?"

He answers, "Madam, if you farted just touching it, you're going to shit your pants when I tell you the price."

* * *

A prostitute went to the doctor complaining of morning sickness. The doctor says, "Congratulations, you're pregnant! Do you know who the father is?"

"Doc," the prostitute replied, "if you ate a can of beans, would you know which one made you fart?"

* * *

A guy goes to pick up his date for the evening. She's not ready yet, so he has to sit in the living room with her parents. He has a bad case of gas and needs to relieve some pressure. Luckily, the family dog jumps on the couch next to him. He decides that he can let a little fart out and if anyone notices, they'll blame the dog.

He farts and the woman yells, "Skipper, get down from there."

The guy says to himself, "Great, they think the dog did it."

He farts again, and the woman again yells for the dog to get off the couch. This goes on for a couple more farts. Finally the woman yells, "Dammit Skipper, get down before he shits on you."

* * *

A philosopher, a mathematician, and a blonde all go to hell and receive a challenge from Satan: if they can stump him, Satan will send them to heaven. The philosopher goes first and asks Satan a devilishly hard philosophy question, to no avail. Satan has the answer.

Next the mathematician asks Satan a question about an impossibly hard theory, to no avail. Satan has the answer.

Next it's the blonde's turn. She pulls up a chair, drills three holes in it, sits down, and farts. "Now Satan," she asks, "which hole did the fart come out of?"

"That's easy," shouts Satan, "all three!"

Looking triumphant she says, "No! It came out of my butthole!"

FUN FACT:
ORIGINS OF THE WORD "SHIT"

In the early Internet days, an urban legend credited the word "shit" to nineteenth-century sailors who loaded manure into boats and—in the interest of making a long and unfunny story much shorter—discovered the hard way that manure and seawater produce methane gas, which is explosive. A few dead seamen later, manure loaders started labeling their ships S.H.I.T., an acronym for "ship high in transit," referring to the fact that manure should be stored on higher decks to avoid contamination with sea water.

Or so the urban legend goes.

The truth is that "shit" has been around a long time, showing up in written works as both a noun and a verb as far back as the fourteenth century. It's a derivative of the Old English words *scite* and *scitte* (meaning "dung" and "diarrhea," respectively), and the Indo-European root *skei-*, meaning "to cut" (so it's distantly related to modern words such as schism and science). For most of history "shit" was spelled "shite" (and is still pronounced that way in parts of Ireland and the United Kingdom). The shortened four-letter version made its first written appearance in the late 1700s.

Can't get enough of shit? Add *History of Shit* to your reading list. The book is by Dominique Laporte, a post-Marxist French psychoanalyst who died at age thirty-five in 1984 (think of the many fascinating tomes denied the world by Laporte's early death). His main argument here is that the management of human waste is the driving force behind both our identities as modern individuals and the development of capitalism. (If you think about it, the man has a point.)

* * *

Two men are in a public bathroom, in adjoining stalls. One man calls over to the other, "Hey, there's no toilet paper in this stall, do you have any over there?"

The second man replies, "No, sorry, I don't have any, either."

The first man asks, "Well, do you have a newspaper?"

The second man says, "No, sorry."

The first man pauses then asks, "Do you have change for a twenty?"

* * *

The teacher asks little Johnny to use the word "definitely" in a sentence. Little Johnny replies, "Teacher, do farts have lumps in them?"

The teacher replies, "Of course, not Johnny."

To which Johnny replies, "Then I definitely have shit my pants."

* * *

Two guys are in a locker room when one notices the other has a cork stuck up his ass. He asks, "How'd you get a cork stuck in your ass?"

The other guy replies, "I was walking along the beach and tripped over a lamp. There was a puff of smoke, and then a genie in a turban popped out. He said, 'I am the genie of the lamp, I can grant you one wish.'

"And I said, 'No shit.'"

* * *

Two statues, one male and one female, stood in a park facing each other. One day an angel appeared and said, "Since the two of you have been exemplary statues and have brought enjoyment to many people, I grant you the gift of life. You have thirty minutes to do whatever you desire."

The two statues instantly came to life and smiled at each other, then ran off into the nearby bushes. The angel smiled as he listened to the two statues giggling, twigs rustling, and bushes shaking. After fifteen minutes, the two statues emerged, satisfied and smiling.

Puzzled, the angel looked at his watch and said, "You still have fifteen minutes."

The male statue looked at the female statue and asked, "Do you want to do it again??"

The female statue said, "Of course! But this time you hold the pigeon down and I'll shit on its head."

* * *

A man walks into a store and says to the salesman, "I want to buy some toilet paper."

"What color?" he asks.

"Give me white," the man says. "I'll color it myself."

* * *

A local store was sending out bathroom supplies as a promotion. About a week later two friends were discussing the latest giveaway. "So what did you think of the toilet brush?"

"Well, it's okay," the friend replied, "but I think I like toilet paper better."

* * *

A child walks in to the living room and asks, "Dad, where does poo come from?"

Without wanting to be too explicit the father replies, "Well, first Mommy makes us dinner. Then we eat it. Then the body takes away all the goodness from the food to make us strong. Then we sit on the toilet. What's left comes out as poo."

Looking horrified the child asks, "But Dad, what about Tigger and Eeyore??"

* * *

Q: What's invisible and smells of worms?
A: Bird farts.

Q: What happened to the blind skunk?
A: He fell in love with a fart.

Q: What happened to the two flies resting on a toilet seat?
A: One got pissed off.

Q: What did the maxi-pad say to the fart?
A: You are the wind beneath my wings.

Q: What's invisible and smells like carrots?
A: Easter Bunny farts.

Q: How can you tell when a moth farts?
A: It flies in a straight line.

Q: What sort of farts do you get by mixing beans and onions?
A: Tear gas.

* * *

Two old men sat eating breakfast one morning. One of the old men noticed something odd in his friend's ear. "Hey, did you know you've got a suppository in your left ear?"

His friend replied, "I do? A suppository?"

He pulled it out and said, "I'm glad you saw this thing. Now I know where my hearing aid is."

* * *

A girl was riding the elevator down to the lobby. The elevator stopped on the tenth floor and a totally cute boy walked in. She farted. Thinking fast on her feet she said, "Cool ringtone, isn't it? Want me to send it to you?"

* * *

A very snobby woman was sitting in a restaurant. As the waiter served the main course she let loose a loud fart that made everyone turn and look. Trying to save face, she said to the waiter, "Sir! Please stop that immediately."

"Certainly, madam," replied the waiter. "Which way was it headed?"

* * *

A man walked into a public toilet, sat down, and dropped his pants in one of the vacant stalls. Out of nowhere, a voice from the next stall said, "Hey, how are you doing?"

The man thought it was a bit strange, but didn't want to be rude. "Not too bad, thanks."

After a short pause, the voice from the next stall said, "So, what are you up to?"

Again the man answered, somewhat reluctantly, "Just having a quick shit. How about you?"

The voice from the next stall said, "Sorry, I'll have to call you back. Some asshole in the next stall is replying to everything I say."

* * *

Q: Why do men fart more frequently than women?
A: Because women don't stay quiet long enough to build up the pressure.

Q: How many men does it take to change a roll of toilet paper?
A: Nobody knows. It's never happened.

Q: Did you hear about the constipated accountant?
A: He couldn't budget.

Q: Did you hear about the constipated mathematician?
A: He worked it out with a pencil.

Q: Did you hear about the constipated *Wheel of Fortune* player?
A: He wanted to buy a bowel.

Q: What did the operator say to the man calling the incontinence hotline?
A: Good afternoon! Can you hold, please?

* * *

A drunk staggered into a church and sat down in a confessional booth, saying nothing. The priest coughed to attract his attention, but the drunk said nothing. The impatient priest knocked on the wall three times to catch the man's attention.

The drunk replied, "No use knocking. There's no paper in this one, either."

* * *

Q: What's dumb?

A: Directions on toilet paper telling you how to use it.

Q: What's dumber than that?

A: Reading them.

Q: What's even dumber still?

A: Reading them and learning something.

Q: What's dumbest of all?

A: Having to correct something that you've been doing wrong.

* * *

Q: Why is pea soup more special than mashed potatoes?

A: Because anyone can mash potatoes.

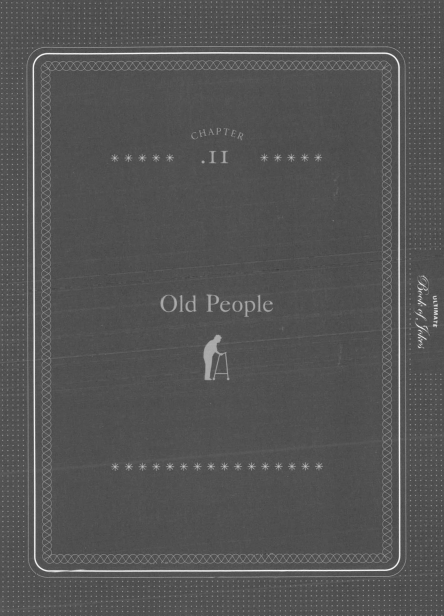

CHAPTER

***** .II *****

Old People

****

CHAPTER 11

Old People

IT DOESN'T MATTER HOW YOUNG YOU ARE. The sad truth is that one day you, too, will be old. Incontinent. Forgetful. You may have a full complement of teeth now. Maybe you have a great memory for people and faces and where you left your car keys. Yet unless you're lucky enough to be squashed by a bus or taken down by a fast-moving cancer, your inevitable fate is a slow and painful old age.

Cheer up, though. Being old is hilarious, especially to the people around you.

* * *

An elderly man with Alzheimer's walks into a bar and notices a rather sexy elderly woman sitting alone at the bar. He saunters over, sits beside her, and says, "Do I come here often?"

* * *

Q: Grandma, were you on Noah's ark?
A: No.
Q: Then how did you survive the flood?

Q: Where can men over the age of sixty find younger, sexy women who are interested in them?
A: In a bookstore, under fiction.

Q: How can you avoid worrying about your wrinkles?
A: Take off your glasses.

Q: Where do old people look for fashionable glasses?
A: On their foreheads.

Q: What is the best thing about being a hundred?
A: No peer pressure.

Q: As people age, do they sleep more soundly?
A: Yes, but usually in the afternoon.

Q: How can you increase the heart rate of your eighty-year-old husband?
A: Tell him you're pregnant.

Q: Why should old people always use valet parking?
A: Valets don't forget where they park your car.

Q: What is the most common remark made by old people in antique stores?
A: "I remember these."

* * *

Johnny asked his grandma how old she was. Grandma answered, "Thirty-nine and holding."

Johnny thought for a moment and then said, "How old would you be if you let go?"

* * *

PATIENT: Doctor, is it common for sixty-year-olds to have problems with short-term memory storage?

DOCTOR: The problem is not storing memory. The problem is retrieval.

* * *

PATIENT: Doctor, my wife is going through menopause. What can I do?

DOCTOR: Finish your basement if you're handy with tools. When you're done you'll have a place to live.

* * *

Grandma and Grandpa were losing their memories, so I told them to take a memory class. The instructor was a famous poet who taught them all sorts of clever word associations to boost their recall. "Who was the instructor?" I asked Grandpa.

"What's the flower that poet wrote about, you know, that one that smells so sweet?"

"A rose?" I asked.

"That's it!" Grandpa shouted. Then he turned to Grandma and said, "Hey Rose! What's the name of that guy who teaches the memory class?"

* * *

Grandpa keeps telling me to fall in love with a girl with small hands. I finally asked him, "Why small hands?"

"Because it will make your penis look larger."

* * *

I asked Grandma how Grandpa was doing. She told me, "He's forgetting names and faces. He even forgets to pull his zipper up. I'm worried about what happens next."

"What, he'll forget to take his pills?" I asked.

"No! He'll forget to pull his zipper down."

* * *

Grandma is a real talker. She loves to pull me aside and give advice. Unfortunately she's also losing her memory. Last night she pulled me aside and left me there.

* * *

Grandpa was sitting on a park bench when a policeman walked by and asked, "Why are you crying?"

Grandpa said, "I'm in love with a twenty-year-old woman. She's smart, sexy, and rich!"

"There now," said the policeman, "there's no need to cry about it."

"Sure there is! I forget where we live."

* * *

Just before the funeral, the undertaker asked a very elderly widow, "How old was your husband?"

"Ninety-eight," she replied. "He was two years older than me."

"So you're ninety-six," the undertaker commented. "Hardly worth going home, isn't it?"

* * *

I'm getting worried about Grandma and Grandpa. Yesterday I asked Grandma, "What is two plus two?"

She answered, "Friday."

Then I asked Grandpa, "What is two plus two?"

He answered, "Twelve."

Then Grandma piped up, "Wait a minute, I know the answer. Two plus two equals four."

"Great!" I said. "How'd you figure it out?"

Grandma said, "Easy. Just subtract twelve from Friday."

* * *

Bernie was eating dinner at a friend's house. The friend prefaced every request to his wife with a sweet term of endearment: honey, darling, sweetheart, precious. When the wife left the room for a moment, Bernie turned to his friend and said, "You're such a sweet old fool. After all the years you've been married, it's a fine thing to keep calling your wife all those pet names."

"To tell the truth," his friend replied, "I forgot her name seven years ago."

* * *

Three retirees, each hard of hearing, were sitting together on a park bench. One man said, "Sunny today, isn't it?"

"No," the second man replied, "it's Thursday."

The third man jumped in, "Me too. Let's have lemonades."

* * *

Grandpa was a famous fighter pilot in World War II. One day his grandson's teacher invited him to share a few war stories with the first-grade class. "This one time," grandpa said, "I was flying back to my air base, and then a Fokker got on my tail, and he just would not let me alone. That stupid Fokker wouldn't get off my tail."

The teacher interrupted and said, "Now children, just to be clear, he's talking about a type of airplane called a Fokker."

"No, lady," grandpa said. "That Fokker was flying a Messerschmitt."

* * *

A ninety-year-old man is having his annual checkup. The doctor asks him how he is doing.

"I've never been better!" the old man replies. "I have an eighteen-year-old bride who is pregnant with my child! What do you think about that?"

The doctor considers this for a moment and says, "I know a guy who is an avid hunter. He never misses a season. But one day, he is in a hurry and he accidentally grabs his umbrella instead of his gun. So he walks in the woods and spots a deer hiding in the brush. He raises his umbrella, points it at the deer, and squeezes the handle. BANG. The deer drops dead in front of him."

GETTING OLD SUCKS.
AND IT'S EXPENSIVE.

Here's something that'll make you gag on your dentures. Throughout retirement, a typical sixty-five-year-old couple (without serious health issues) will need about $200,000 simply to pay for out-of-pocket medical costs. Include the cost of nursing home care and that same elderly couple needs a $260,000 cash pile to survive the so-called golden years. (Almost makes you want to put granny and grandpa out on the street, or watch 'em sail gently into the sunset on an ice floe . . .)

And that's just the tip of the iceberg. Here's a list of what to expect as you climb the rungs of the old-age ladder:

∾ Your heart gets less efficient as you age, working harder to pump the same amount of blood through your body. Your blood vessels lose elasticity and hard fatty deposits form on the inner walls of your arteries. Sooner or later you'll know how to properly spell and pronounce "atherosclerosis."

∾ Your bones shrink in size and density as you age. No joke—you may become shorter in your old age. Less dense bones are also susceptible to fracture, while your muscles, tendons, and joints generally lose strength and flexibility. Think of the old guy walking down the street with a hunch, limp, and cranky attitude.

∾ Swallowing and the flow of digested food through your intestines slow down as you age. You may never notice these changes directly. But you might notice more constipation. Cheers.

∾ About 10 percent of people sixty-five and older experience a loss of bladder control (hello, incontinence!). Women are more likely than men to have incontinence.

∾ The number of neurons in your brain decreases as you age, and your memory becomes spotty. Your reflexes tend to become slower, and you're less coordinated and have difficulty with balance.

∾ With age, your eyes are less able to produce tears, your retinas thin, and your lenses gradually turn yellow and become less clear. You're also more likely to get cataracts, glaucoma, and macular degeneration.

∾ Even if you've spent your life brushing and flossing, as you age your mouth will feel drier and your gums will recede. Your teeth will darken slightly and become more brittle.

"That's impossible!" the old man says. "Somebody else must have shot that deer."

The doctor nods in agreement, "Exactly."

* * *

On hearing her elderly grandfather passed away, Jane went straight to her grandparents' house to comfort her ninety-five-year-old grandma. When Jane asked how Grandpa had died, her grandma said, "He had a heart attack while we were making love."

Horrified, Jane told her grandmother that having sex when you're nearly a hundred years old was surely asking for trouble.

"Oh no, my dear," Grandma replied. "Many years ago, realizing our advanced age, we figured out the best time to do it was when the church bells would start to ring. It was just the right rhythm. Nice, slow, and even. In on the 'ding' and out on the 'dong.'"

Grandma paused, and then added, "And if that damn ice cream truck hadn't come along, he'd still be alive today."

* * *

Two Wal-Mart greeters were sitting on bench during their break. One turned to the other and said, "I'm seventy-five years old and I'm just full of aches and pains. I know you're about my age, how do you feel?"

The second man said, "I feel great, just like a newborn babe."

"Really? A newborn babe??"

"Yup. No teeth. No hair. And I think I just wet my pants."

* * *

"Look at me!" boasted a fit old man to a group of young people. "Each morning I do fifty push-ups, fifty sit-ups, and then walk two miles. I'm fit as a fiddle!"

"How do you do it?" one of the youngsters asked.

"Well, I don't smoke. I don't drink. I don't stay up late. And I don't chase after women! Thanks to all this clean living, tomorrow I'm going to celebrate my ninety-fifth birthday!"

"Oh, really?" a skeptical onlooker asked. "How?"

* * *

When my grandfather was ill, my grandmother used to rub lard on his back. After that, he went downhill quickly.

* * *

A police officer pulled over an elderly woman for speeding while driving her husband to an appointment. The officer tried to explain the reason he pulled her over, but she kept turning to her husband asking, "Eh? What did he just say?"

Finally the husband replied, "He said he stopped you for speeding."

The officer asked the woman for her driver's license and she turned and asked her husband, "What did he say?"

The husband replied, "He wants to see your driver's license."

The women handed the officer her license, and he noticed she was from Brownsville. The officer told the couple he remembered the town well, because he had the worst sexual experience of his life in Brownsville. The woman looked at her husband and asked, "What did he say?"

The husband replied, "He says he knows you."

* * *

A thirty-five-year-old woman visited a plastic surgeon, who told her about a new procedure called "the knob." A small knob is placed on top of a woman's head. The knob can be turned to tighten up skin and produce the effect of a new facelift.

Of course the woman wanted it. Over the course of many years, the woman tightened the knob and remained young and vibrant looking.

After thirty years, the woman returned to the surgeon. "All these years, everything has been working just fine," the woman said. "I've had to turn the knob many times and I've always loved the results. But now I've developed two problems. First, I have these terrible bags under my eyes and the knob won't get rid of them."

The doctor looked at her closely and said, "Those aren't bags under your eyes, those are your breasts."

She said, "Well, I guess there's no point asking about the goatee."

* * *

Two men are sitting next to each other on a crowded downtown bus. The first man notices the second man has his eyes closed. "Hey, what's the matter?" he asks. "Are you sick?"

"No, I'm okay," the second man replies. "It's just that I hate to see old ladies standing."

* * *

For the first time in many years, an old man traveled from his rural home to the city in order to see a movie. After buying his ticket, he stopped at the concession stand to purchase popcorn. Handing the attendant $3.50, he couldn't help but comment, "The last time I came to the movies, popcorn was only twenty-five cents."

"Well, sir," the attendant replied, "you're really going to enjoy yourself. The movies come with sound now."

* * *

An old man was driving on the freeway and his mobile phone rang. His wife was on the line, her voice thick with anxiety. "Howard! I just saw on the news there's a car driving the wrong way on the freeway. Please be careful!"

"One?" replied Howard. "You've got to be kidding me. I see at least a hundred!"

* * *

Two old men go to a brothel. The madam asks what they'd most like to experience. "Well, ma'am, we'd both like to spend the evening with a woman."

"How old are you, gentlemen?"

One of the men replies, "We're twin brothers, born the same day, and we just turned ninety-five."

The madam tells one of the working girls to take the brothers upstairs and put each of them in a room with a blow-up doll. So the men go upstairs and do their thing. When they come back downstairs one of the brothers asks the other, "So how was it?"

"Not so good," his brother replied. "I think the girl was dead. She just lay there. How was yours?"

"I think mine was a witch," the brother replied.

"A witch??"

"Yeah. I bit her on the tit and she farted then flew out the window."

* * *

An old man went to a brothel and asked the madam if he could spend the night with a young girl. Surprised, she asked how old he was. "I'm ninety years old," he replied proudly.

"Ninety!" the madam exclaimed. "Don't you realize you've had it?"

"Oh, sorry," the old man said. "How much do I owe you?"

* * *

A distraught older woman called her doctor. "Is it true," she asked, "that the medication you prescribed has to be taken for the rest of my life?"

"Yes, I'm afraid so," the doctor told her.

There was a moment of silence before the woman asked, "I'm wondering, then, just how serious is my condition? This prescription is marked 'No refills.'"

* * *

An old man was living out his days at a nursing home. One day the nurse noticed he was sad and depressed. She asked, "Is there anything wrong?"

"Yes, nurse," the old man said, "my private part died today, and I am very sad."

Knowing her patients were sometimes a little senile, she replied, "Oh, I'm so sorry, please accept my condolences."

The next day, the old man was walking down the hall with his penis hanging out of his pajamas. The nurse pulled him aside gently and said, "You shouldn't be walking down the hall like that Please put your private part back inside your pajamas."

"But nurse," the old man protested, "I told you yesterday that my private part died."

"Yes, you did tell me that. But why is it hanging out of your pajamas?" the nurse asked.

"Well," he replied, "today is the viewing."

* * *

An old man went to his doctor for a routine checkup. The doctor asked him about his sex life.

"Well," the old man said, "it's not bad at all, to be honest. My wife ain't all that interested anymore, so I just cruise around looking for action. In the past week I had sex with three total strangers in a park."

"At your age!" the doctor said. "I hope you at least take some precautions."

"Doc, I may be old but I ain't stupid!" the man said. "I gave 'em all a phony name."

* * *

Two old men are sitting on the front porch of their retirement home. One man turns to the other and asks, "Do you still get horny?"

"Oh yes, sure I do."

"What do you do about it?" the first man asks.

"I usually suck a lifesaver or two," the second man replies.

After a few moments the first man asks, "Who drives you to the beach?"

* * *

An old man walks into a pharmacy and says to the pharmacist, "I need some Viagra."

"No problem at all," the pharmacist replies. "How many pills do you need?"

"Just a few," the old man says, "but can you cut each one into four small pieces?"

"No sir, that won't do you any good," the pharmacist warns. "You need a full dose in order to have sex comfortably."

"Sex?! I'm over eighty-five years old!" the old man replies. "I don't need them for sex. I just want my penis to stick out far enough so I don't pee on my damn shoes."

* * *

Grandpa recently turned sixty-five and went to the doctor for a complete physical. After an exam the doctor said grandpa was doing "fairly well" for his age. Grandpa was a little concerned and asked, "Doc, do you think I'll live to eighty?"

The doctor asked, "Do you smoke tobacco or drink alcohol?"

"Oh no," Grandpa replied, "and I don't do drugs, either."

"Do you have many friends and entertain frequently?"

Grandpa said, "No, I usually stay home and keep to myself."

"Do you eat beef and pork?"

"No, my other doctor said red meat is unhealthy!"

"Do you spend a lot of time doing things in the sun, like playing golf, sailing, or bicycling?"

"No, I don't."

"Do you gamble, drive fast cars, or have lots of sex?"

"No, I don't do any of those things anymore."

The doctor looked at Grandpa and said, "Then why do you care?"

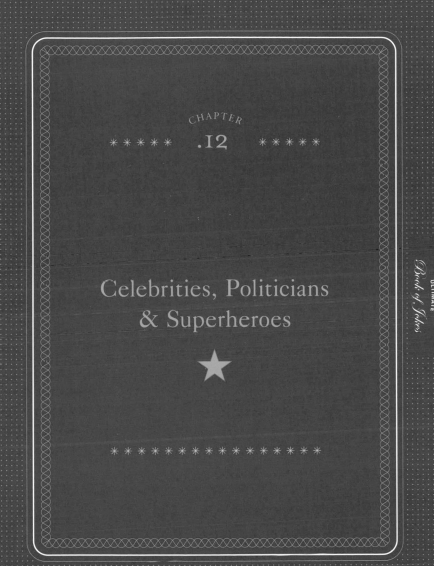

CHAPTER

***** .12 *****

Celebrities, Politicians
& Superheroes

★

****

Celebrities, Politicians & Superheroes

NO JOKE: FARRAH FAWCETT AND MICHAEL JACKSON died on the very same day in 2009. When Farrah died they dimmed the lights on Broadway. When Michael died they dimmed the lights at Toys 'R' Us. Ouch.

It's tough to be famous in America (or anywhere else, for that matter). One minute people love you, can't get enough of you. The next minute you're fodder for late-night comedians and *People* magazine exposés. Just ask O. J. Simpson, Tiger Woods, Madonna, and Minnie Mouse.

* * *

Q: What was Dick Van Dyke's given name?

A: Penis Van Lesbian.

Q: What did Arnold Schwarzenegger say when asked if he has ever used steroids?

A: "I once put one in my mouth. But I never swallowed."

Q: Why will Mike Tyson never file for bankruptcy?

A: Without pictures, he's not sure if he can make it to Chapter 11.

Q: Why did Kobe Bryant buy a dictionary?

A: To learn what part of "no" he doesn't understand.

Q: Why do Mike Tyson's eyes water during sex?

A: It's the pepper spray.

Q: What is Sammy Davis Jr.'s favorite television show?

A: *Queer Eye for the Straight Guy.*

* * *

A little boy asks his dad, "Daddy, is God a man or a woman?"

"Both, son, God is both."

A few minutes later the little boy asks his dad, "Daddy, is God black or white?"

"Both son, both," the dad replies.

"Daddy, does God love children?"

"Yes son, he loves all children."

A few minutes later the little boy asks, "Daddy, is Michael Jackson God?"

Q: What's the difference between Michael Jackson and a plastic bag?
A: One is white, plastic, and dangerous to young children. The other is a plastic bag.

Q: How does Michael Jackson know it's time for bed?
A: When the big hand is on the little hand.

Q: Why did Michael Jackson place a phone call to Boyz II Men?
A: He thought it was a delivery service.

Q: What's the worst stain to try to remove from little boy's pants?
A: Michael Jackson's makeup.

Q: What did Michael Jackson say to Lorena Bobbit?
A: "Silly Bobbit! Dicks are for kids!"

Q: Why did Michael Jackson get food poisoning?
A: He ate twelve-year-old nuts.

Q: What did Michael Jackson order at the Chinese restaurant?
A: Sum Yung Boy.

* * *

Michael Jackson walked out from the operating room after his wife gave birth to their son. Michael asked the doctor, "Hey doc, how long till we can have sex?"

The doctor replied, "At least wait until he is walking, Michael."

* * *

Q: What's worse than Tiger Woods driving your Cadillac Escalade?
A: Dick Cheney riding shotgun.

Q: What's Tiger Wood's favorite club?
A: The nightclub.

Q: What's the difference between a car and a golf ball?
A: Tiger Woods can drive a golf ball four hundred yards.

Q: What's the difference between Santa Claus and Tiger Woods?
A: Santa always stops after three hos.

Q: What's the main reason Santa Claus is so jolly?
A: He knows where all the bad girls live.

* * *

Q: What do JFK Jr. and a penguin have in common?
A: They're both kinda cute, but neither one can fly.

Q: What's the difference between Elvis and JFK Jr.?
A: Elvis was bloated *before* he died.

Q: Why didn't JFK Jr. shower before the plane flight?
A: He figured he would wash up on shore.

Q: What does JFK Jr. miss most about Martha's Vineyard?
A: The runway.

Q: What was JFK Jr. drinking when his plane crashed?
A: Ocean Spray.

Q: How did JFK Jr. learn how to fly?
A: He took a crash course.

Q: What are the three most common causes of death in America?
A: Heart disease, cancer, and being a Kennedy.

* * *

Q: What is O. J. Simpson's Web site address?
A: Slash slash backslash escape.

Q: Why can't you invite O. J. Simpson over for Thanksgiving?
A: Because he's always cutting up all the white meat.

Q: Everybody knows O. J. Simpson is a slicer. So how does he round out his golf foursome?
A: With Monica Lewinsky (hooker), Ted Kennedy (can't drive over water), and Bill Clinton (can't get it in the hole).

* * *

A boy asked his father, "Dad, what's the difference between *potentially* and *realistically*?"

The father thought for a moment and answered, "Go ask your mother if she would sleep with Brad Pitt for a million bucks. Then ask your sister and brother is they'd each sleep with Brad Pitt for a million bucks. Come back and tell me what you've learned."

So the boy asked his mother, "Mom, would you sleep with Brad Pitt for a million bucks?"

His mother replied, "Of course! We could really use the money to fix up the house and pay for your education."

The boy asked his sister the same question and she answered, "Oh my God oh my God! I love Brad Pitt, I'd sleep with him in a second. The million bucks is just icing on the beefcake."

The boy then asked his brother, who replied, "Of course I would, you dumbass. I could really use the money."

The next day the boy's father asked, "So did you find out the difference between *potentially* and *realistically*?"

"Yes, I did," the boy answered. "Potentially, you and I are sitting on three million bucks, but realistically, we're living with two hookers and a homo."

* * *

Q: What was the last thing Kurt Cobain said to Courtney Love?
A: "Hole is gonna be really big."

Q: Why does Snoop Dogg carry an umbrella?
A: Fa' drizzle.

Q: What's the opposite of Christopher Reeve?
A: Christopher Walken.

Q: How many sugars does Christopher Reeve take in his coffee?
A: *Blinks twice*

Q: What do Barbie and Britney Spears have in common?
A: Both are blonde, brainless, and made out of plastic.

Q: Why is the movie *Gigli* banned in Baghdad?
A: The Baghdaders can't take any more bombs.

Q: What do Dale Earnhardt and Pink Floyd have in common?
A: Their greatest hit was *The Wall*.

Q: What's the difference between Jesus and Madonna?
A: Jesus was only resurrected once.

Q: How were Angelina Jolie and Madonna paid for hosting the Hope for Haiti concert?
A: In orphans.

Q: What happened to the kids when Jon and Kate Gosselin got divorced?
A: Madonna got them.

Q: Why didn't Ken and Barbie ever have kids?
A: Ken came in a different box.

* * *

Q: How is duct tape like the Force?
A: It has a dark side, a light side, and it binds the galaxy together.

Q: How did Darth Vader know what Luke was getting for Christmas?
A: He felt his presents.

Q: What did Obi-Wan say to Luke at the Chinese restaurant?
A: "Use the forks, Luke."

Q: Which *Star Wars* character works at a restaurant?
A: Darth Waiter.

* * *

Sean Connery was being interviewed on Australian television. He bragged that, despite being in his seventies, he could still have sex four times a night. Kylie Minogue was also a guest, and she looked intrigued. After the show Kylie said, "Sean, if I am not being too forward, I'd love to have sex with an older man. Let's go back to my hotel."

So they go back to her hotel and have great sex. Afterward Sean says, "If you think that was good, let me sleep for fifteen minutes and we can have even better sex. But while I'm sleeping, hold my balls in your left hand and my penis in your right."

Kylie looks a bit perplexed but agrees. After fifteen minutes Sean Connery wakes up and they have even better sex. Then Sean says, "Kylie, that was wonderful. But if you let me sleep for an hour, we can have the best sex yet. Just hold my balls in your left hand and my penis in your right."

The results are mind-blowing. Once it's all over, and the cigarettes are lit, Kylie asks, "Sean, does my holding your balls in my left hand and your dick in my right stimulate you while you're sleeping?"

"No," Sean replies, "but the last time I slept with a slut from Australia, she stole my wallet."

* * *

Mickey Mouse was in the middle of a nasty divorce with Minnie Mouse. The judge said, "I'm sorry, Mickey, but I can't grant you a divorce on the grounds that Minnie is mentally insane."

"I didn't say she was mentally insane," Mickey said in a huff. "I said she was fucking Goofy."

* * *

Superman is flying faster than a speeding bullet, feeling kinda horny. He sees Batman and stops to ask him if he knows of any superheroes who'd be willing to have sex with him. "Absolutely—Wonder Woman is great in bed," Batman tells him.

"I don't know," Superman says, shaking his head. "I've known Wonder Woman for years, it might be awkward."

Superman flies off and sees Spider-Man hanging around. "Hey, Spider-Man. I'm feeling horny. You know any superheroes I can have sex with?"

"Sure! Call Wonder Woman, she's easy—and she's great in bed."

"I can't!" Superman says. "She's an old friend, I can't do it."

Superman flies off and, a few minutes later, notices Wonder Woman with her legs spread apart on the roof of a tall building. He thinks, "Hmmm, maybe Batman and Spider-Man are right. Maybe I should have sex with Wonder Woman."

So he swoops down, faster than a speeding bullet, and has his way with her in two seconds flat, then flies off.

Wonder Woman looks up and says, "What was that?"

"I don't know," the Invisible Man says, "but my ass hurts."

* * *

Two men were drinking at a bar on the twenty-first floor of a downtown building. The first man said, "I bet you fifty bucks I can jump out that window and come straight back in."

The second man said, "You're on!"

The first man jumped out the window and disappeared for a second before jumping straight back in. Disappointed about losing $50, the second man said, "I'll bet you a hundred bucks you can't do that trick again."

Sure enough, the first man jumped out the window and disappeared for a second, before jumping straight back in. Thinking he must have caught a freak gust of wind, the second man said, "Okay, I bet you two hundred bucks that I can jump out the window and come straight back in, just like you."

The first man said, "Okay, you're on!"

The second man jumped out the window and fell to his death. The bartender walked over to the first man shaking his head and said, "Gee, you can be a real asshole when you're drunk, Superman."

* * *

Q: Why is Superman stupid?
A: Because he wears underwear over his pants.

Q: Why is Batman stupid?
A: Because he wears underwear over his pants, plus a belt over his underwear.

Q: Why is Wonder Woman stupid?
A: Because she wears a belt on her head.

Q: Why is Spider-Man stupid?
A: Because he wears underwear on his head.

* * *

A drunk walks out of a bar and sees a nun standing at a bus stop. He walks over and punches her in the face. She falls to the ground and he kicks her, screaming, "You're not so tough tonight, are you, Batman!"

* * *

Q: What did Batman say to Robin before they got into the Batmobile?
A: "Get into the Batmobile, Robin."

Q: How can Batman defeat the Joker?
A: With a handful of sleeping pills.

* * *

Q: What's the difference between David Carradine and Heath Ledger?
A: Nothing, now.

Q: What's the difference between Heath Ledger and Heath Ledger jokes?
A: The jokes will get old.

* * *

Q: Who's supporting INXS on their latest tour?
A: The Stranglers.

Q: Why did Michael Hutchence stay at the Ritz-Carlton when in Sydney?
A: Because it's a cool place to hang out.

Q: Why was Paula Yates attracted to Michael Hutchence?
A: Because he was well hung.

Q: Why did Bob Geldof take up karate?
A: He heard he could kill Michael Hutchence with a black belt.

Q: What does Michael Hutchence have that Bob Geldof doesn't?
A: A widow.

Q: What's the difference between Michael Hutchence and Princess Di?
A: Michael Hutchence used his belt.

* * *

Q: What was Princess Diana wearing when she died?
A: A blue bonnet.

Q: Why did Microsoft rename Windows in honor of Princess Diana?
A: Because Windows looks equally flash, consumes vast amounts of resources, and crashes spectacularly.

* * *

St. Peter met Mother Teresa at the gates of heaven and said, "You have been a fine example to mankind. I'm giving you a nice halo." Mother Teresa was honored.

Later, as Mother Teresa was walking around heaven, she saw Princess Diana and was surprised the Princess's halo was so large. Mother Teresa went back to St. Peter to complain. "I spent my life helping the poor and sick. Princess Diana was worthy, certainly, but she was nowhere near as charitable as me. So why does she have a larger halo?"

"That's not a halo," St. Peter replied. "That's a steering wheel."

* * *

Q: What was Elton John's tribute song for Michael Hutchence?
A: *Dangle in the Wind.*

Q: What was Elton John's tribute song for Mother Teresa?
A: *Sandals in the Bin.*

Q: What was Elton John's tribute song for John Denver?
A: *Cessna in a Spin.*

* * *

A man walked into the doctor's office. "Doc, I can't stop singing 'Green, Green Grass of Home.'"

"That sounds like Tom Jones's syndrome," the doctor replied.

"Is it common?" the man asked.

"It's not unusual," the doctor answered.

Q: Why doesn't Chuck Norris wear a condom?
A: Because there is no such thing as protection from Chuck Norris.

Q: What can Chuck Norris do, according to Einstein's Theory of Relativity?
A: Roundhouse-kick you, yesterday.

Q: What's the quickest way to a man's heart?
A: Chuck Norris's fist.

Q: Why won't Chuck Norris ever have a heart attack?
A: His heart isn't foolish enough to attack him.

Q: Why is Chuck Norris suing MySpace?
A: For taking the name of what he calls everything around you.

Q: Why did Chuck Norris kill Jesus?
A: Because Jesus smoked the last cigarette.

* * *

Q: How does Ozzy Osbourne change a lightbulb?

A: First, he bites off the old one.

Q: How long does it take Terri Schiavo to change a lightbulb?

A: We don't know. The lazy bitch won't get out of bed.

Q: What is the best thing about getting a blow job from a Spice Girl?

A: Ten minutes of silence.

Q: Why is Stevie Wonder always smiling?

A: He doesn't know he's black.

Q: What happened when Richard Simmons had plastic surgery to remove his love handles?

A: They removed his ears by mistake.

* * *

A priest was getting a haircut at a Washington DC barbershop. After his haircut the priest asked, "How much?"

"No charge," the barber said. "I consider it a service to my Lord." The next morning, the barber found a Bible with a thank-you note from the priest.

The next day a policeman was getting his haircut and asked, "How much?"

"No charge," the barber said. "I consider it a service to my community." The next morning, the barber found a box of doughnuts and a thank-you note from the policeman.

The next day, a senator was getting his haircut and asked, "How much?"

"No charge," the barber said. "I consider it a service to my country." The next morning, the barber found six more senators waiting in line.

* * *

Q: Why did Senator Larry Craig miss the stimulus package vote?
A: He was in the men's room, introducing his own package.

Q: What's the best way to close the U.S. prison camp at Guantánamo Bay?
A: Turn it into a bank.

Q: What do golf and Florida elections have in common?
A: Low score wins.

* * *

A young boy asks his dad, "What is politics?"

"Well, son," the dad answers, "let me explain it this way: I'm the breadwinner of the family, so let's call me capitalism. Your mom, she's the administrator of the money, so we'll call her the government. We're here to take care of your needs, so we'll call you the people. The nanny, we'll consider her the working class. And your baby sister, we'll call her the future. Now, think about that and see if that makes sense."

So the boy goes off to bed. Later that night he hears his baby sister crying, so he gets up and finds that his sister's diaper is full of poo. The little boy goes to his parents' room and sees his mother sound asleep. Not wanting to wake her, he goes to the nanny's room. Finding the door locked, he peeks in the keyhole and sees his father having sex with the nanny. He gives up and goes back to bed.

The next morning the boy says to his dad, "I think I understand the concept of politics now."

"Good," the dad says. "Tell me in your own words what you think it's about."

The boy replies, "While capitalism is screwing the working class, the government is sound asleep, the people are being ignored, and the future is in deep shit."

* * *

Q: How will everyone remember Bill Clinton in history?
A: The president after Bush.

Q: What's Bill Clinton's idea of safe sex?
A: When Hillary is out of town.

Q: What did Chelsea say when Hillary asked if she had sex yet?
A: "Not according to Dad."

Q: Would you have sex with Bill Clinton?
A: Eighty percent of the survey respondents said "Not again."

Q: What did Bill Clinton say when asked to sign a hotly contested abortion bill?
A: "I don't need to sign it, just go ahead and pay it."

Q: Why did Monica Lewinsky switch parties and join the Republicans?
A: Because the Democrats left a bad taste in her mouth.

* * *

Jimmy Carter, Richard Nixon, and Bill Clinton were on a holiday cruise together when the ship suddenly started to sink. Jimmy Carter yelled, "Quick, save the women and children!"

Richard Nixon shouted, "Screw the women and children."

Bill Clinton asked, "Do we have time?"

YOUR CONSTITUTIONAL RIGHT TO LAUGH AT POLITICIANS

Political satirist may be the second-oldest profession in the world (milliseconds after hooker, no doubt). Political zingers go back thousands of years. The Greek playwright Aristophanes filled his comedies with barbed jabs at the influential citizens of Athens. In the fourteenth century Dante's *Divine Comedy* featured prominent political figures in hell. And let's not forget about Mark Twain, who wrote in the nineteenth century, "Suppose you were an idiot and suppose you were a member of Congress. But I repeat myself."

Political humor is all about shining a spotlight on the incompetence and foibles of political leaders. The butts of jokes are typically not amused, but in America, thanks to the First Amendment, political satire is liberally interpreted and widely protected.

Consider the 1988 Supreme Court case of Larry Flynt vs. Jerry Falwell. *Hustler* magazine publisher Larry Flynt printed a ruthless (and ruthlessly funny) parody of televangelist Jerry Falwell, who considered it libelous and sued. A jury awarded Falwell $150,000 for emotional distress. But the Supreme Court unanimously overturned the decision on First Amendment grounds. Go, Larry, go!

Ultimately, successful politicians learn to embrace the satire instead of fight it. They also learn to give as good as they get. Cue Bill Clinton, who was brutally "humorized" during his presidency, poking fun at Barack Obama at the 2010 Gridiron Dinner in Washington DC:

"I said, 'Mr. President, what's up?'"

"And President Obama said, 'Hi Bill, I'm just here in the White House polishing my Nobel Peace Prize.'"

"He asked me, 'Bill, you got one of these yet?'"

"And I said, 'No, no I don't.'"

"'No? Well, Jimmy's got one.'"

"I said, 'Yes, yes he does.'"

"'And Al Gore, he's got two, I think . . .'"

"I said, 'Yes Mr. President, he sure does; wears 'em around his neck.'"

* * *

Four presidents were caught in a tornado and transported to Oz. They entered Emerald City and came before the Great Wizard, who asked, "What brings you to Oz?"

Jimmy Carter stepped forward and said, "I've come for some courage."

"Granted! Who is next?"

Ronald Reagan stepped forward and said, "Well, I'm told I need a heart."

"Granted! Who is next?"

George W. Bush stepped forward and said, "He-he, I'm told that I need a brain."

"Granted! Who is next?"

After a long silence, Bill Clinton stepped up but didn't say a word. The Wizard asked, "Well, go on, tell me what brings you to Oz?"

Bill Clinton looked around the room and said, "Uhh, is Dorothy here?"

* * *

A cannibal walked into a restaurant and looked over the menu.

Tourist: $3
Broiled Missionary: $5
Baked Explorer: $15
Grilled Democrat or Republican: $50

The cannibal called the waiter over and asked, "Why such a price difference for the grilled politicians?"

The cook replied, "Have you ever tried to clean one? They're so full of shit, it takes all morning."

* * *

Q: How many Republicans does it take to change a lightbulb?
A: None. If liberals would just leave it alone, it would change itself.

* * *

The war against terror was going badly for Osama bin Laden. So Osama himself decided to send President Bush a letter. Bush opened the letter, which contained a single line of secret code: 370H-SSV-0773H.

President Bush was baffled, so he emailed it to the Department of Defense. They couldn't decipher the code, so they sent it to the FBI. No one at the FBI could make sense of it, so it was sent to the CIA. The best CIA code breakers couldn't decipher the message, either.

Eventually the President's advisors posted full-page ads in newspapers around the world, asking Osama bin Laden to clarify his statement.

The next day Osama bin Laden released a follow-up letter: "Tell your president he's holding the message upside down."

* * *

Donald Rumsfeld was giving George W. Bush a military briefing about Iraq. "Mr. President, I have some unfortunate news. Yesterday three Brazilian soldiers were killed in battle."

"Holy shit, Don!" the president cried out. "That's awful news. That's going to be a public-relations nightmare. My God, Don, it could bring down my presidency! We can't tell anybody about this."

"Mr. President," a confused Rumsfeld replied, "I agree this is bad news, but it's not going to destroy your presidency."

The president burst into tears and buried his head into his hands. "Okay, Don, I trust your judgment on this. Just tell me, how many is a brazillion?"

* * *

George W. Bush and Dick Cheney walked into a diner. A waitress handed them menus and asked if they were ready to order. Bush looked over the menu and said, "Honey, can I have a quickie?"

The appalled waitress stormed off. Cheney leaned over to Bush and whispered, "George, it's pronounced 'quiche.'"

* * *

George W. Bush went to the doctor for the results of his brain scan. The doctor said, "Mr. President, I have bad news for you. First, we've discovered that your brain has two sides: a left side and a right side."

Bush interrupted, "Well, isn't that normal? I thought everybody had two sides to their brain."

"That's true," the doctor replied. "But Mr. President, your brain is unusual. On the left side there isn't anything right, and on the right side there isn't anything left."

* * *

George W. Bush wanted to buy a puppy for his daughters. A breeder with a litter of puppies was summoned to the White House. Bush looked them over and asked, "Are they all Republicans?"

The breeder said, "Yes, Mr. President, they were all born Republicans."

President Bush said he needed to talk it over with Laura, and asked the breeder to come back the following week.

A week later, the breeder returned with the puppies. George and Laura looked them over, and Laura asked, "So you're certain, these puppies are all Republicans?"

"No, ma'am," the breeder answered. "These puppies are all Democrats."

An annoyed President Bush said, "Last week, you told me these puppies were all Republicans. What happened?"

"Well, Mr. President, since then the puppies have opened their eyes."

* * *

An old lady calls 911. When the operator answers she screams, "Help! Send the police right away! There's a damn Democrat on my front porch and he's playing with himself."

"What?" the operator asked. "Did you say a Democrat was masturbating on your front porch?"

"That's exactly what I said!" the old lady shouted. "Please send the police!"

"Well," the operators asked, "how do you know he's a Democrat?"

"You damn fool!" the old lady said. "If he was a Republican, he'd be screwing somebody else."

* * *

Q: How old is John McCain?
A: He remembers when Joe Biden was bald.

Q: How old is John McCain?
A: His Social Security Number is XXXIV.

Q: How old is John McCain?
A: His Secret Service code name is "The Clapper."

Q: How old is John McCain?
A: His passport photo is signed by Van Gogh.

Q: How old is John McCain?

A: When his plane was shot down over enemy lines he shouted, "Damn you, Red Baron!"

* * *

John McCain woke up screaming. His wife, Cindy, was used to the senator having flashbacks of Vietnam. "Are you okay?" she asked.

"I am now," said McCain. "I was having a terrible nightmare."

Cindy asked, "What happened this time? Tell me about it."

"I was in a crowded place, surrounded by throngs of people," McCain said. "They were all jabbering at me in some language I couldn't understand. I wanted to tell them something, but I couldn't collect my thoughts, and I couldn't articulate. I was just frozen, like a deer in the headlights."

"Oh, John," said Cindy. "Stop thinking about last night's presidential debate and get some sleep."

* * *

Q: How dumb is Sarah Palin?

A: She thinks the Kyoto Accord gets slightly better gas mileage than a Honda.

Q: How dumb is Sarah Palin?

A: She thinks the capital of China is Chinatown.

Q: How dumb is Sarah Palin?

A: She prefers DirectTV to Kabul.

Q: How dumb is Sarah Palin?

A: She thinks soy milk is Spanish for "I am milk."

Q: How dumb is Sarah Palin?
A: She ordered Bear Stearns as an appetizer.

Q: How dumb is Sarah Palin?
A: She thinks billboards are postcards from giants.

* * *

A teacher asked her class how many were fans of Barack Obama. All the kids raised their hands except one boy. The teacher asked the boy why he didn't raise his hand. "I'm not a Barack Obama fan. I'm a George Bush fan."

The teacher asked, "What makes you a George Bush fan?"

"Because my mom's a George Bush fan and my dad's a George Bush fan," the boy said. "So that makes me a George Bush fan."

The teacher wanted all of her kids to think for themselves, so she asked the boy, "What if your mom was an idiot and your dad was a moron, what would that make you?"

The boy said, "That would make me a Barack Obama fan."

* * *

Q: What would you get if you crossed Albert Einstein with Barack Obama?
A: $E = MC$ Hammer.

Q: Why won't Barack Obama laugh at himself?
A: It would be racist.

Relationships

★★★★★★★★★★★★★★★

CHAPTER 13

Relationships

THE PSYCHOANALYST ERICH FROMM FAMOUSLY WROTE, "Love is the only sane and satisfactory answer to the problem of human existence." Clearly, the tormented characters in this chapter would benefit from sixty minutes on Erich Fromm's couch.

The truth is that where there is love, there is pain. The pain of unrequited love and the pain of watching your true love grow old, fat, and farty. The pain of heartbreak and the pain of discovering your wife having sex with the pool man. The pain of separation and the pain of breaking a nail while holding the pillow over your ex-husband's face.

Does love mean never having to say you're sorry? Yes, up until the moment when the judge asks how you'd like to plead.

* * *

Q: Why is it so hard for women to find men who are sensitive, caring, and good-looking?

A: Because those men already have boyfriends.

Q: How many honest, intelligent, and caring men in the world does it take to do the dishes?

A: Both of them.

Q: What's the difference between a singles bar and a circus?

A: At a circus, the clowns don't talk.

Q: How are men and parking spots alike?

A: The good ones are always taken and the ones that are left are handicapped.

Q: How does a man plan for his future?

A: He buys two cases of beer, instead of one.

Q: What did God say after he created man?

A: I can do way better than this.

Q: How do you know God is a man?

A: If God was a woman, semen would taste like chocolate.

Q: What do a clitoris, an anniversary, and a toilet have in common?

A: Men always miss them.

* * *

A husband says coyly to his wife, "Darling, let's swap positions tonight."

"Great idea!" the wife replies. "Tonight, you stand in front of the sink and do the dishes and I'll sit in front of the TV and fart."

* * *

After a quarrel, a husband says to his wife, "You know, I was a fool when I married you."

"Yes, dear," she replies. "But I was in love and didn't notice."

* * *

A man said to his wife, "Honey, let's go out and have some fun tonight."

"Okay," she replied. "Please leave the porch light on if you get home before I do."

* * *

Q: What does it mean when a man is in your bed gasping for breath and calling your name?
A: You didn't hold the pillow down long enough.

Q: Why are almost all serial killers men?
A: Because women prefer to kill one man slowly over many, many years.

Q: What do you call a woman who knows where her husband is every night?
A: A widow.

* * *

An efficiency expert concluded his lecture with a note of caution. "You don't want to try these techniques at home without preparing carefully and thinking through all the possible outcomes."

"Why not?" an audience member asked.

"Well, I studied my wife's breakfast routine for many years," the expert explained. "She made multiple trips between the refrigerator, the counter, the stove, the pantry, and the dishwasher, typically carrying just a single item at a time. One day I said to her, 'Honey, why don't you try carrying several items at once and save yourself some time?'"

"And did it save time?" the audience member asked.

"Actually, yes, it did," the expert replied. "It used to take her twenty-five minutes to make breakfast. Now I do it in nine."

* * *

A man walks into a flower shop and says, "I need some flowers."

"Of course," the florist says, "what do you have in mind?"

"I'm not really sure."

The florist says, "Let me ask that a different way. What exactly have you done?"

* * *

Q: How can you tell if a man is sexually excited?
A: He's breathing.

Q: How many men does it take to screw a lightbulb?
A: Five. One to do the screwing, and four to listen to him brag.

Q: What happens to men who mix Viagra and Prozac?
A: They're ready to go, but not sure where.

Q: Why is a theme park like Viagra?
A: In both cases you wait three hours for a two-minute ride.

Q: Why is sleeping with a man like a soap opera?
A: Just when it starts to get interesting, it's over until next week.

Q: What's the difference between a bachelor and a married man?
A: A bachelor comes home, sees what's in the refrigerator, and goes to bed. A married man comes home, sees what's in bed, and goes to the refrigerator.

* * *

Dave and Greg are talking about Freudian slips and how embarrassing they can be. Greg recalls the time he was at the airport with his wife, buying plane tickets to Pittsburgh, and mistakenly asked the large-chested blonde behind the counter for "two pickets to Tittsburgh."

They chuckle, and Dave shares his own story. "We were sitting at the dinner table, and I meant to ask my wife to pass the butter. But instead I said, 'Thanks for ruining my life, you fucking bitch.'"

* * *

A group of women are on vacation when they see a hotel with a sign that reads "For Women Only." They are traveling without boyfriends and husbands, so they decide to check it out. An attractive man at reception explains how it works. "We have five floors. Go up floor by floor, and once you find what you are looking for, you can stay there. It's easy to decide since each floor has a sign telling you what to expect."

So the women walk up to the first floor and find a sign that says "All the men on this floor are short and plain."

The women laugh and move on to the next floor, where they find a sign that says "All the men here are short and handsome." The women are intrigued but decide to keep going.

On the third floor they find a sign that says "All the men on this floor are tall and plain." The women are impressed, but still keep going.

On the fourth floor the sign says "All the men here are tall and handsome." The women are thrilled and are about to go in, when they realize there is still one floor left. Wondering what they are missing, they head up to the fifth floor.

There they find a sign that says "There are no men here. This floor was built to prove there is no way to please a woman."

* * *

An airplane is about to crash, when a female passenger stands up and announces, "If I'm going to die, I want to die feeling like a woman."

She removes all her clothes and shouts, "Is there somebody on this plane who is man enough to make me feel like a woman?"

A man stands up, removes his shirt, and says, "Here, iron this!"

* * *

A husband and wife were having an argument. "You're going to be sorry! I'm going to leave you," she threatened.

The husband replied, "Make up your mind, which is it?"

* * *

Q: Did you hear about the bulimic bachelor party?
A: The cake came out of the girl.

Q: What food sucks 80 percent of the sex drive from a woman?
A: The wedding cake.

Q: How are women and rocks alike?
A: You skip the flat ones.

Q: What's the difference between a woman and a battery?
A: Batteries have a positive side.

Q: How are women and tornadoes alike?
A: When they come they're wet and wild, when they leave they take the house and car.

Q: Did you hear about the guy who finally figured out women?
A: He died laughing before he could tell anybody.

Q: What do women and carpets have in common?
A: If you lay them right the first time, you can walk all over them later.

Q: Why do women close their eyes during sex?
A: No woman wants to see a man enjoying himself.

Q: What's the difference between mad cow disease and PMS?
A: Nothing.

Q: Why do only 10 percent of women go to heaven?
A: Because if they all went, it would be hell.

Q: How many women with PMS does it take to screw in a lightbulb?
A: One. And do you know why it only takes one? Because you don't know how to change a lightbulb. You didn't even notice it burned out. In fact, you would sit in the dark for a week before even noticing! And when you did finally notice, you wouldn't know where to find a new lightbulb even though they've been stored in the same cabinet for ten years. And even if by some miracle you actually found the new lightbulb, a week later the chair you dragged over to stand on would be in the same damn spot.

* * *

A man walked into a bar and said, "Bartender, pour me a triple scotch and keep 'em coming!"

"That's a tall order, mister. What's the matter?" the bartender asked.

"My wife and I got into a fight," the man explained. "And now she isn't talking to me for a whole month."

The bartender paused and said, "I don't know about you. But if my wife stopped talking to me for a month, I'd be thrilled."

"Exactly!" the man said. "Today's the last day."

* * *

Q: What's the difference between love, true love, and showing off?
A: Spit, swallow, and gargle.

Q: What's the best thing about dating homeless girls?
A: You can drop them off anywhere.

Q: What is the difference between a pregnant woman and a lightbulb?
A: You can unscrew a lightbulb.

Q: Why did God create alcohol?
A: So ugly women can have sex, too.

* * *

A woman wakes up in the middle of night and hears her husband crying like a baby. "What's wrong?" she asks.

"Honey, remember how twenty years ago I got you pregnant? And your dad said if I didn't marry you, he'd have me thrown in jail?"

"Yes, of course, but why is that making you cry now?"

"Because I would have been released today."

* * *

A man walks up to a woman in a bar and says, "Do you want to dance?"

The woman looks him over and says, "I don't really like this song, and even if I did, I wouldn't dance with you."

The man says, "I'm so sorry, you must have misunderstood me. I said you look fat in those pants."

* * *

I was talking to my wife the other day about reincarnation. She asked me, "What actually is reincarnation?"

I said to her, "Honey, it's when you die and come back as something completely different."

"So I could come back as a pig?" she asked.

I said, "Honey, you're not listening to me, are you?"

* * *

A couple is at the marriage counselor's office, and the husband asks his wife, "Darling, have you ever cheated on me?"

The wife sheepishly admits, "Yes, I have, three times. The first time was when we needed money to send the kids to college. Remember the banker who refused our loan but then came to the house?"

The husband was angry, but also touched.

"The second time was when we needed money for your open-heart surgery. Remember the doctor who refused to operate but then came to the house?"

The husband was angry yet also genuinely moved. "And the third time?" he asked.

"Remember how you wanted to be president of the school board but were a dozen votes short?"

* * *

A man sticks his head into a barbershop and asks, "How long before I can get a haircut?"

The barber looks around the busy shop and says, "About an hour." The man leaves.

A few days later the same man sticks his head in the door and asks, "How long before I can get a haircut?"

The barber looks around at the busy shop and says, "Same as the other day, about an hour." The man leaves.

A week later the same man sticks his head in the shop and asks, "How long before I can get a haircut?"

The barber looks around the shop, which isn't very busy, and says, "About ten minutes." The man leaves.

The barber looks over at a friend and says, "Hey, follow that guy and see where he goes. He keeps asking how long he has to wait for a haircut, but never comes back."

A little while later the friend comes back into the barbershop chuckling. The barber asks, "So, where did he go when he left here?"

"Your house!" the friend answers.

* * *

The marriage counselor asked her client, "Did you wake up grumpy this morning?"

"No, I let him sleep in."

* * *

After thirty years of marriage, a wife finds a secret drawer in her husband's closet. It contains two golf balls and $500. She confronts her husband and asks for an explanation.

"Every time I was unfaithful to you," he explains, "I put a golf ball in the drawer."

She figures two infidelities in thirty years isn't too bad. "But what about the five hundred dollars?" she asks.

"Well," he says, "whenever I got a dozen golf balls, I sold them for cash."

* * *

A woman found a slip of paper in her husband's coat pocket with the words "Jamie Lee" written on it. She confronted her husband, who explained, "It's the name of a horse I bet on last week."

The very next day, the wife asked her husband for a divorce. "Why are you doing this?" the distraught husband asked.

His wife replied, "Because this morning your horse called and left a message."

FUN FACT:
DIVORCE RATES

Those whom God hath joined together, let no man put asunder.

It sounds nice when invoked at weddings. Yet in America an astounding 54 out of every 100 marriages ends in divorce. No surprise, America leads the world in divorces. It's partly due to how easily divorces are granted (think: no-fault divorce laws). And it's partly due to the lack of an enforced waiting period (for example, in Italy, it takes a minimum of three years for divorces to be final; in the U.S. a few weeks is more common).

Within the U.S. it's no surprise Nevada grants more divorces than any other state (c'mon—if you get married on a whim by Elvis, divorces better be quick and easy). Rounding out the top five are Arkansas, Oklahoma, Tennessee, and Wyoming. Much-maligned California ranks a middling 32 out of 50.

On the flipside is Japan, where fewer than 2 in 100 marriages end in divorce. Ditto Armenia, Italy, and Macedonia, all of which see fewer than 10 divorces in 100 marriages.

* * *

Two friends are hunting in the woods when one says to the other, "Hey, I can see your house from here. And your wife is in the bedroom with some guy!"

The distraught husband says, "Please, I need you to shoot her in the head. And then shoot him in the nuts."

"Easy," the friend says. "I can make that in one shot."

* * *

A husband said to his wife, "Honey, I have a confession to make. I've been seeing a psychiatrist."

"That's okay, dear," the wife replied. "I've been seeing the pool man and our daughter's basketball coach."

* * *

After being with his blind date for what seemed like eternity, a man took a call on his cell phone. Earlier, he had secretly arranged to have a friend call him so he would have an excuse to leave if something like this happened.

When he hung up the phone, he put on a grim expression and said, "I have some bad news. My grandfather just died."

"Thank heavens," his blind date replied. "If yours hadn't, mine would have had to."

* * *

Q: What's the longest sentence in the English language?
A: I do.

Q: What's the definition of divorce?
A: The future tense of marriage.

Q: If first marriages are triumphs of imagination over intelligence, what are second marriages?
A: Triumphs of hope over experience.

Q: What is the only thing divorce proves?
A: Whose mother was right in the first place.

Q: Why are divorces so expensive?
A: Because they're worth it.

Q: Did you hear about the new "Divorce Barbie"?
A: It comes with all of Ken's stuff.

* * *

A man and wife were in divorce court, arguing over the custody of their children. The mother told the judge that, since she brought the children into this world, she should retain custody. The man also wanted custody of his children, so the judge asked for his justification.

After a long silence, the man replied, "Your Honor, when I put a dollar in a vending machine and a Coke comes out, does the Coke belong to me or to the machine?"

* * *

A farmer walked into a lawyer's office and said, "I want to get one of those dee-vorces."

The lawyer said, "Okay, but do you have any grounds?"

The farmer said, "Yeah, I got about a hundred and forty acres."

The lawyer said, "No, you don't understand, do you have a case?"

The farmer said, "No, I don't have a Case, I have a John Deere."

The lawyer said, "No, no, you still don't understand. I mean do you have a grudge of some kind?"

The farmer said, "Yeah I got a grudge, that's where I park my John Deere."

The lawyer said, "No sir, I mean, do you have a suit?"

The farmer said, "Yes sir, I got a suit. I wear it to church on Sundays."

The frustrated lawyer said, "Listen—does your wife beat you up or anything?"

The farmer said, "No sir, we both get up about five-thirty in the morning."

"Okay, let me put it this way. Why do you want a divorce?" the lawyer asked.

"Well, I can never have a meaningful conversation with her."

* * *

"Mr. Smith, I have reviewed this case very carefully," the divorce court judge said, "and I've decided to give your wife seven hundred dollars a week."

"That's very fair, your honor," the husband acknowledged. "And every now and then I'll try to send her a few bucks, too."

* * *

After being married for thirty years, a man said to his wife, "Honey, do you realize thirty years ago I had a cheap apartment, a cheap car, slept on a couch, and watched a small TV, but I got to sleep every night with a hot twenty-one-year-old blonde? Now we have a nice house, a nice car, a big bed, and a wide-screen TV, but I'm sleeping with a fifty-one-year-old blonde. It seems to me you are not holding up your side of things."

The wife, a very reasonable woman, replied, "Honey, go out and find a hot twenty-one-year-old blonde, and I'll make sure you once again live in a cheap apartment, drive a cheap car, sleep on a couch, and watch a small TV."

CHAPTER

***** .14 *****

Dirty Naughty Things

****

Dirty Naughty Things

BLOW JOB! PENIS! LESBIANS! Let's not mince words. This chapter's theme is "sex," be it straight, gay, kinky, or otherwise.

A joke book without dirty jokes is unfathomable. While the world's oldest recorded joke is about farts, the *second oldest* recorded jokes are about a naked goddess exposing her vagina and a bored pharaoh looking for action along the Nile. (I'm not making this up—check out the "Ye Olde Guffaws" chapter!)

Clearly sex cuts across all eras, all races, all social classes. It's a root desire, pardon the pun, and a powerful force that's shaped every aspect of mankind's history on earth. No surprise, then, that sex jokes are ubiquitous and remain, even today, one of the most common categories of humor. Like it or not, sex and naughtiness occupy prime seats in the joke pantheon.

* * *

One day God said to Adam, "I've got some good news and some bad news. Which do you want first?"

Adam asked for the good news first. God smiled benignly and said, "I've created two new organs for you. One is called a brain. The brain gives you intelligence, allowing you to create new things and to have meaningful conversations with Eve. The other organ is called a penis. The penis allows you to reproduce and begin populating the planet. The penis will bring you great physical pleasure."

Adam was thrilled. "God, these are wonderful gifts you have given me. What could possibly be the bad news?"

God looked at Adam and said with great sorrow, "The bad news is, I only gave you enough blood to operate one of these organs at a time."

* * *

A Jehovah's Witness knocks on the door of a house. The door is opened by a twelve-year-old boy holding a cocktail, smoking a cigarette, and wearing his mother's nightgown. The startled Jehovah's Witness says, "Um, is your mom or dad home?"

The boy replies, "What the hell do you think, mister?"

* * *

It was the first day of school. Two boys arrived late to class and the teacher asked the first boy, "Why are you tardy?"

"I've been on Blueberry Hill," the boy answered.

The teacher then asked the second boy the very same question. He replied, "I was on Blueberry Hill, too."

As the boys sat down a girl arrived late to class. "Let me guess," the teacher said, "you were on Blueberry Hill, too?"

"No," the girl said, "I am Blueberry Hill."

* * *

A young man goes into a drugstore to buy condoms. The pharmacist explains that condoms come in packs of three, nine, or twelve and asks which the young man prefers. "I've been with this girl for a while now," the boy says to the pharmacist. "She is really hot, and I think tonight is the night. We're having dinner with her parents, and then we're going out. I've got a feeling we'll have sex after that, and after she's had sex with me once, she'll want to have sex with me again and again. I better take the twelve-pack."

Later that night, the boy sits down to dinner with his girlfriend and her parents. He asks if he might say grace and they agree. He begins the prayer and continues praying for several minutes.

His girlfriend leans over and whispers, "You never told me you were so religious."

The boy leans over and whispers, "You never told me your dad was a pharmacist."

* * *

A high school biology teacher asked her class, "What part of the human body increases to nine times its normal size when excited?"

"That's disgusting!" a young girl replied, blushing. "I don't have to answer that question!"

One of the boys in the class raised his hand and said, "That's easy, it's the pupil of the eye."

The teacher said to the boy, "That's correct." Then the teacher turned to the girl and said, "I have three things to say to you, young lady. First, you didn't do your homework. Second, you have a dirty mind. And third, you're in for a big disappointment."

* * *

Q: When does a Cub Scout become a Boy Scout?
A: When he eats his first brownie.

* * *

A young boy was taking a sex ed class. The teacher drew a penis on the chalkboard and asked, "Does anybody know what this is?"

The boy answered, "Of course, I do. My dad has two of them."

"Two?" the teacher asked with arched eyebrows.

"Yeah, two," the boy replied. "A small one for peeing and a big one for brushing the babysitter's teeth."

* * *

A young man took a blind date to the carnival. "What do you want to do first?" he asked her.

"I want to get weighed," she said. So they walked over to the weight guesser.

Next they went on the Ferris wheel. When the ride was over, the young man again asked what she would like to do. "I want to get weighed," she said. So back to the weight guesser they went.

Afterward they walked around the carnival until the young man asked her again, "What do you want to do now?"

And again she answered, "I want to get weighed."

By this time, the young man assumed his date was a nut job and took her home. Once inside, the girl's roommate asked, "So, how did your blind date go?"

The girl replied, "Oh, it was wousy."

* * *

A husband and wife are in bed. The husband is feeling frisky and asks if she's in the mood. His wife answers, "Sorry, not tonight, dear. I have a headache."

The man asks, "Is that your final answer?"

"Yes, dear, I'm not joking. I have a terrible headache. It's my final answer."

"Okay, then," the husband says, "I'd like to phone a friend."

* * *

A man is walking through the hotel lobby on the way to a reception. On the way he accidentally bumps into a woman and inadvertently jabs his elbow into her breast. Thinking fast, the man turns to her and says, "Miss, if your heart is as soft as your breast, I know you'll forgive me."

"Sir," the women replies, "if your penis is as hard as your elbow, I'm in room 210."

* * *

Q: What's the speed limit of sex?
A: Sixty-eight. Because at 69 you have to turn around.

Q: What's the square root of 69?
A: Ate something.

Q: What's the square root of 6.9?
A: A good thing screwed up by a period.

Q: What's the difference between erotic and kinky?
A: Erotic is using a feather. Kinky is using the whole chicken.

Q: What's the difference between "oooh!" and "aaah!"?
A: About three inches.

Q: What's the difference between light and hard?
A: You can sleep with a light on.

Q: What do a Rubik's Cube and a penis have in common?
A: The more you play with them, the harder they get.

Q: What do you call a bunny with a crooked penis?
A: Fucks funny.

Q: What's the definition of a Yankee?
A: Same thing as a "quickie" only you do it yourself.

Q: What do you get when you cross a penis and a potato?
A: A dicktator.

Q: What's long, hard, and full of seamen?
A: A submarine.

Q: What's the difference between sin and shame?
A: It's a sin to put it in. It's a shame to pull it out.

Q: What did the depressed penis say to the psychiatrist?
A: "Doc, I'm surrounded by nuts and my neighbor's an asshole."

Q: What happens if you take Viagra and Rogaine at the same time?
A: You have a stiff, hairy penis.

Q: What did the penis say to the condom?
A: "Cover me, I'm going in."

Q: Why do midgets laugh when they run?
A: Because the grass tickles their balls.

Q: What is the difference between snowmen and snowwomen?
A: Snowballs.

Q: What has a hundred balls and screws old ladies?
A: Bingo.

Q: What are the two main problems about being an egg?
A: You only get laid once and the only woman to sit on your face is your mother.

* * *

A chicken and an egg are together in bed. The chicken is smoking a cigarette with a satisfied smile, while the egg is frowning and looking slightly annoyed. The egg mutters, "Well, I guess that answers that old riddle."

* * *

Two eggs are boiling in a pot. The female egg says, "Look, I've got a crack."

"No use telling me," the male egg replies, "I'm not hard yet."

* * *

One morning a woman walks out her front door and notices a strange little man at the bottom of her garden. "You're a goblin," she says. "I caught you and now you owe me three wishes!"

The goblin replies, "Fair enough, you caught me. What's your first wish?"

The woman thinks for a moment and says, "I want a huge house with a garden to live in."

"Okay, done," the goblin says.

"My second wish is a sports car."

"Okay, done," the goblin says.

"My last wish is a million dollars!"

"Okay, done," the goblin says. "But to make your wishes come true you must have sex with me all night long."

"Okay," the woman says, "if that's what it takes."

The next morning the little man wakes the woman up. "Tell me," he asks, "how old are you?"

"I'm twenty-five," she replies.

"Fuck me," says the little man. "Twenty-five and you still believe in goblins?"

* * *

Two dwarfs walk into a bar, where they pick up two prostitutes and take them back to adjacent hotel rooms. Unfortunately the first dwarf can't get an erection no matter what. He's depressed, and his depression is made worse by the fact that, from the next room, he hears cries of, "One, two, three—uuuh!" all night long.

In the morning the second dwarf asks the first, "How was your night?"

"It was so embarrassing. I simply couldn't get a hard-on."

The second dwarf shook his head. "You think that's embarrassing? I couldn't even get on the fucking bed."

* * *

Q: What's better than a rose on your piano?
A: Tulips on your organ.

Q: What is better than a cold Bud?
A: A warm bush.

Q: What should you do if your girlfriend starts smoking?
A: Slow down. And possibly use a lubricant.

Q: What's the definition of eternity?
A: The time between when you cum and when she leaves.

Q: What is the definition of "making love"?
A: Something a woman does while a guy is fucking her.

Q: Why don't men perform oral sex on women the morning after sex?
A: Have *you* ever tried pulling apart a grilled cheese sandwich?

Q: Which sexual position produces the ugliest children?
A: Ask your mom.

Q: What's the difference between Bigfoot and your mom?
A: Your mom is better in bed.

Q: What is it when a man talks dirty to a woman?
A: Sexual harassment.

Q: What is it when a woman talks dirty to a man?
A: $4.99 a minute.

* * *

A teacher says to her students, "Today we're learning multisyllable words. Who has an example of a multisyllable word?"

A boy in the front row raises his hand. "Okay," the teacher says, "tell me your multisyllable word."

The boy stammers, "Mas-tur-bate."

The teacher smiles and says, "Wow, that's a real mouthful."

The boy says, "No ma'am, you're thinking of a blow job."

SEX IS FUNNY, UNTIL YOU HAVE KIDS

Laugh all you want to about sex. One day you may have kids of your own. And then it won't be so funny.

That's because kids around the world are losing their virginity at earlier ages than ever before. Based on a 2007 global study (by a condom maker—no kidding!), the average age kids have sex for the first time is 17.3.

Kids from Iceland have sex before anybody else (15.6), followed by the Germans (15.9), Swedes (16.1), and Danes (16.1). In the middle are Americans (16.4), British (16.6), and French (16.8). At the other end of the spectrum are Malaysians (19.0), Indonesians (19.1), Vietnamese (19.6), and—three cheers for the world's oldest virgins!—Indians (19.8).

More sobering is this trend: kids continue to have sex at an earlier age than previous generations. Kids aged 25 to 34 lost their virginity at an average age of 17.9; kids aged 21 to 24 averaged 17.5; and kids aged 16 to 20 averaged just 16.3.

The only bright spot is that kids these days are better protected. According to the study, today's youth are eight times more likely to use condoms than their grandparents were at the same age. The trailblazers here are the Dutch: in Dutch public schools kids learn how to put a condom on a dildo by age 12.

* * *

A boy brings his girlfriend home after a night out together. At the front door he leans with one hand on the wall and says to her, "Hey, why don't you give me a blow job?"

"What?" she says. "You're crazy. No."

"Don't worry," the boy says. "It will be quick, no problem."

"No! Somebody might see us."

"Not at this time of night," the boy replies.

"I said no, and I mean it."

"C'mon, just a quick blow job. Please . . . "

Just then the girl's younger sister opens the door, rubbing her eyes. "Hey, Dad says either you have to blow him, I have to blow him, or he will come down himself and give the guy a blow job. But for God's sake, tell your boyfriend to take his goddamn hand off the intercom."

* * *

A man wearing a ski mask walks into a sperm bank, holding a gun. He says to the receptionist, "Open up the vault or I'll blow your head off."

"But sir," the receptionist cries, "it's just a sperm bank!"

"I don't care," the man shouts, "open the vault now!"

The receptionist opens the vault. Inside there are dozens of sperm samples. The man says, "Take one of those sperm samples and drink it."

"But sir, these are sperm samples!"

"I don't care," the man shouts, "drink one!"

The receptionist knocks one back. "Another, drink another!" the man screams.

After the receptionist drinks a half-dozen sperm samples, the man takes off his ski mask and says, "See, honey. It's not that hard."

* * *

A family of prostitutes is chatting at the end of a long day. The daughter says, "Today I got twenty-five dollars for a blow job."

The mother sighs and says, "In my day it was five dollars."

The grandmother sighs and says, "In my day we were just glad for a warm drink."

* * *

A man walks into a bar and orders five shots of bourbon. As he sets up the glasses the bartender asks, "So what's the special occasion?"

The man answers, "My first blow job."

"Your first blow job? Let me pour you another shot on the house!" the bartender offers.

"Sure, thanks," the man replies. "Anything to get the nasty taste out of my mouth."

* * *

A man limps into a bar with a cane and an alligator. The bartender says, "Hang on, you can't bring that animal in here."

"But my gator does a really great trick," the man says.

"Okay," the bartender says, "let's see it."

So the man pulls out his dick and shoves it in the alligator's mouth.

Q: How do you know your girlfriend is too young for you?

A: You have to make airplane noises to get your penis in her mouth.

Q: How can you tell you have a high sperm count?

A: Your girlfriend must chew before she can swallow.

Q: What's the most intelligent thing to come out of a woman's mouth?

A: Einstein's cock.

Q: What's the difference between your paycheck and your cock?

A: You don't have to beg your girlfriend to blow your paycheck.

Q: Which doesn't belong: wife, eggs, or blow job?

A: Blow job. You can beat your wife, you can beat your eggs, but you can't beat a blow job.

Then he bashes the alligator's head with the cane. A crowd gathers around and the entire bar is astonished when the man pulls out his dick without a single scratch. He looks around at the crowd and says, "Does anybody else want to try?"

An old lady raises her hand and says, "Sure, but don't hit me with that stick."

* * *

A newlywed couple are about to have sex for the first time. The bride says to her new husband, "Please be gentle. I'm still a virgin."

The husband is shocked. "How's that possible? This is your fourth marriage!"

"I know," she replies, "it's odd. But my first husband was a gynecologist and all he wanted to do was look at it. My second husband was a psychiatrist and all he wanted to do was talk about it. And my third husband was a stamp collector and all he wanted to do was . . . Oh, how I do miss him."

* * *

Q: Why do men want to marry virgins?
A: Because they can't stand criticism.

Q: Why do men find it difficult to make eye contact?
A: Because breasts don't have eyes.

Q: How is air like sex?
A: It's no big deal unless you're not getting any.

Q: What is the definition of a perfect lover?
A: A man with an eight-inch tongue who can breathe through his ears.

Q: What's the definition of female masturbation?
A: Finishing the job off properly.

Q: What is the difference between golf balls and G-spots?
A: Men spend two hours searching for golf balls.

Q: Why do women rub their eyes when they get up in the morning?
A: Because they don't have balls to scratch.

* * *

A man and a woman are naked in the middle of a dark forest. After a few minutes the man gets up and says, "Damn, I wish I had a flashlight."

The woman says, "Me too. You've been eating grass for the past ten minutes."

* * *

Little Red Riding Hood was walking through the woods. Suddenly the Big Bad Wolf jumped from behind a tree and said, "Little Red Riding Hood, I'm going to screw your brains out."

Little Red Riding Hood calmly reached into her picnic basket and pulled out a gun and aimed it at the wolf. "No you're not," she said. "You're going to eat me, just like it says in the book."

* * *

A newlywed couple are about to have sex for the first time. The man removes his shoes and socks and reveals toes that are twisted and discolored. "What happened to your feet?" his wife asks.

"I had a childhood disease called tolio."

"You mean polio?"

"No, tolio," the husband says. "It only affects the toes."

He then removes his pants and reveals a misshapen pair of knees. "What happened to your knees?" she asks.

"Well, I also had kneesles."

"You mean measles?"

"No, kneesles," the husband says. "It only affects the knees."

He then removes his underpants. His wife says, "Don't tell me, you also had smallcox?"

* * *

Q: What did the banana say to the vibrator?
A: "Why are you shaking? I'm the one she's gonna eat."

Q: What do you call a truck full of dildos?
A: Toys for Twats.

Q: What's the difference between a slut and a bitch?
A: A slut sleeps with everyone. A bitch sleeps with everyone but you.

Q: Why is the space between a woman's breasts and her hips called a waist?
A: Because you could easily fit another pair of tits there.

* * *

A man walks into a bar and orders a beer. The barmaid is extremely attractive and he asks, "Can I buy you a drink?"

The barmaid says, "You've no chance with me, love. I'm a lesbian."

"What's a lesbian?" the man asks.

"You see that blonde at the end of the bar, the one with the big tits?" the barmaid says. "Well, I want to rip off her shirt and suck her nipples."

"Holy shit!" the man says. "I must be a lesbian, too!"

Q: What's the new and politically correct name for lesbian?
A: Vagitarian.

Q: What do you call a lesbian Eskimo?
A: Klondike.

Q: What do you call a lesbian with fat fingers?
A: Well hung.

Q: What do you call 1,000 armed lesbians?
A: Militia Etheridge.

Q: What do you call a lesbian dinosaur?
A: Lickalotopuss.

Q: What do you call a gay dinosaur?
A: Megasaurass.

Q: What do gays and ambulances have in common?
A: They both get loaded from the rear and go "Woo hoo!"

Q: What did the first condom say to the second condom as they walked past the gay bar?
A: "Wanna go get shit-faced?"

Q: Why did the condom fly across the room?
A: Because it was pissed off.

Q: What is the difference between oral sex and anal sex?
A: Oral sex makes your whole day. Anal sex makes your hole weak.

Q: How many gay men does it take to change a lightbulb?
A: Two. One to change it and one to say, "Fabulous."

Q: What did the gay couple say when a condom floated to the surface in the hot tub?
A: "Who farted?"

Q: Did you hear about the gay rabbit?
A: He found a hare up his ass.

Q: Did you hear about the gay truckers?
A: They exchanged loads.

Q: Did you hear about the two gay judges?
A: They kept trying each other.

* * *

A man and a woman were standing in line at the supermarket check-out. The woman's basket had one can of soup, one apple, one pear, one chocolate bar, and one mini tub of ice cream. The man leaned over and said, "You're single, aren't you?"

"How can you tell?" the woman asked.

The man answered, "Because you're ugly as fuck."

* * *

A trucker had been hauling loads for nearly a month. One afternoon he stopped at a brothel and said to the madam, "I've got eight hundred bucks. I want your ugliest woman and a turkey sandwich."

"But sir," the madam says, "for eight hundred dollars you could have any woman in the house and a three-course meal."

The trucker replies, "Honey, I ain't horny. I'm homesick."

* * *

Q: What's green, slimy, and smells like Miss Piggy?
A: Kermit's finger.

Q: Why did Raggedy Anne get thrown out of the toy box?
A: Because she kept sitting on Pinocchio's face screaming, "Lie to me!"

Q: Why does the Easter Bunny always hide the Easter eggs?
A: Because he doesn't want anybody to know he's been screwing the chickens.

Q: How can you pick out Ronald McDonald in a nudist colony?
A: He's the one with sesame-seed buns.

Q: What do you see when the Pillsbury Doughboy bends over?
A: Doughnuts.

Q: How did Burger King get Dairy Queen pregnant?
A: He forgot to wrap his Whopper.

* * *

A man walks into a diner and orders a burger with fries. He notices a small hair when he bites into his burger and says, "Waitress, there's a hair in my hamburger. It's disgusting, what the hell is going on in your kitchen?"

So the waitress takes him into the kitchen, where the man witnesses the cook flatten a raw meat patty under his hairy arm pit. "That's disgusting!" the man screams.

"If you think that's disgusting," the waitress says, "you should see him make donuts."

* * *

A mother and young daughter were walking through a park and saw a couple having sex on a bench. The daughter asked, "Mom, what are they doing?"

The mother paused and said, "They are making cakes."

The next day at the zoo, the daughter saw two orangutans having sex and asked the same question. The mother replied with the same answer, "They're making cakes, dear."

The next day the daughter said to her mother, "Mom, you and Dad were making cakes last night in the living room."

Shocked, the mother asked, "How do you know?"

"Because," the daughter replied, "I licked the icing off the couch."

* * *

Q: What do you call a man at an abortion clinic?
A: Relieved.

Q: Why can't you fool an aborted fetus?
A: Because it wasn't born yesterday.

Q: What's the difference between a television and my pregnant girlfriend?
A: When I put a coat hanger inside my pregnant girlfriend, I didn't get a very good reception.

* * *

Q: Know what the leper said to the prostitute?
A: Keep the tip.

Q: Who makes more money, a drug dealer or a hooker?
A: A hooker, because she can wash her crack and reuse it.

Q: What do bungee jumping and hookers have in common?
A: They both cost a hundred bucks and if the rubber breaks, you're screwed.

Q: What's the difference between an epileptic oyster fisherman and a hooker with diarrhea?
A: One of them shucks between fits.

Q: What did the doctor say to the hooker who complained no hair would grow on her vagina?

A: "Did you ever see grass grow on a highway?"

Q: If young hooker uses Vaseline, what does an old hooker use?

A: Poligrip.

Q: What do you call a Serbian prostitute?

A: Sloberdown Mycockyoubitch.

Q: What do you call a hooker with no legs?

A: A nightcrawler.

Q: What do you tell a hooker with two black eyes?

A: Nothing. You've already told her twice.

* * *

"Mommy, Mommy! I just learned how babies are made. I saw you kissing Daddy's penis last night."

"No silly, that's not how babies are made. That's how Mommy gets her new jewelry."

* * *

"Mommy, Mommy! Why are you sitting naked on top of Daddy?"

"Um, I'm just squeezing the air out of Daddy's tummy."

"Oh, is that because the babysitter keeps blowing up Daddy's penis?"

* * *

"Mommy, Mommy! What's an orgasm?"

"I don't know, dear. Ask your father."

CLASSIC DEAD HOOKER JOKES

Q: How many cops does it take to push a hooker down the stairs?

A: None. She fell.

Q: What's the difference between your job and a dead hooker?

A: Your job still sucks.

Q: Why did the hooker fall out of the tree?

A: Because she was dead.

Q: What's the difference between Jell-O and a dead hooker?

A: Jell-O wiggles when you eat it.

Q: What's the difference between a Corvette and a dead hooker?

A: I don't have a Corvette in my garage.

Q: What do you do if your hooker is screaming and bleeding in your hotel room?

A: Shoot her again.

Q: What's the difference between an onion and a hooker?

A: You don't cry when you chop up a hooker.

* * *

"Mommy, Mommy! Why are you white and I'm black?"

"When I remember that party, honey, you're just lucky that you don't bark."

* * *

A little boy asks his mom, "Mommy, can I take a shower with you and Daddy?"

"Sure, honey. Just don't look up and don't look down, okay?"

The little boy nods and gets in the shower. Then he looks up and says, "Mommy, what are those?"

The mom thinks for a second and says, "Those are Mommy's headlights."

Then the little boy looks down and says, "Daddy, Mommy, what's that?"

The dad thinks for a second and says, "That's Daddy's snake, and that's Mommy's grass."

Later that night the little boy wakes up and says "Mommy, Daddy? Can I sleep with you?"

"Okay, but don't look under the covers," the mom says.

The little boy gets into bed and looks under the covers. "Mommy, Mommy! Turn on your headlights! Daddy's snake is in your grass."

* * *

A little boy and his grandfather are raking leaves in the backyard. The boy finds an earthworm struggling to get back into its hole. "Grandpa," the boy says, "I bet I can put that worm back in its hole."

The grandfather says, "You're on! I'll bet ten dollars you can't. The worm is too limp and fragile, you'll never get it into the hole."

The little boy runs into the house and comes back with a can of hair spray. He sprays the worm until it is straight and stiff as a board. Then he puts the worm back into the hole. The grandfather hands the little boy ten dollars, grabs the hair spray, and walks back into the house.

Five minutes later the grandfather comes back out and hands the boy another ten dollars. The little boy says, "Grandpa, you already gave me ten dollars."

"I know. That was from your grandma."

* * *

An elderly couple was about to have sex in the nursing home's broom closet. The woman decided to warn the man about her heart condition. "You need to know this, I have acute angina," she said.

"That's good news," the man replied, "because you have the ugliest pair of tits I've ever seen."

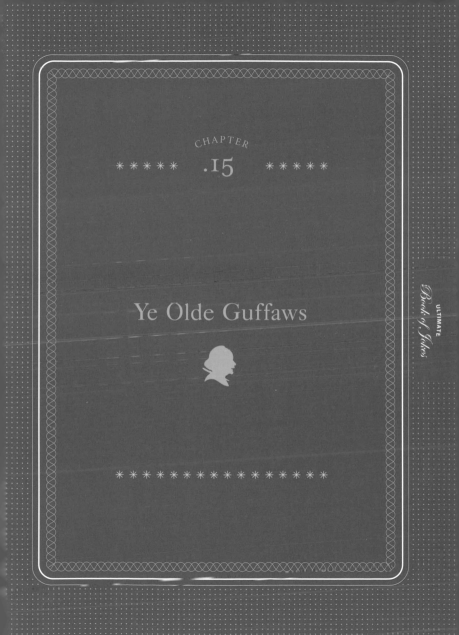

CHAPTER

***** .15 *****

Ye Olde Guffaws

Ye Olde Guffaws

WHETHER YOU'RE AN ANCIENT GREEK PHILOSOPHER, an ancient Egyptian pharaoh, or a Walmart greeter, themes such as adultery, drunkenness, and politics play well on the stage of comedy. And because the themes tend to be universal, many jokes from antiquity age well. You may not know much about Abderites or Thracians, but it's pretty clear they were the bubbas and blondes of their day.

Many of the jokes below are taken from various translations of *Philogelos* ("The Laughter Lover"), a collection of Greek jokes dating from the fifth century AD that is the world's most comprehensive collection of ancient humor. Though to be fair, many of these "jokes" are more like funny anecdotes. I've modernized these ancient guffaws as much as possible, while still trying to retain their ancient zing.

To round things out I've included a few choice quotes from Shakespeare and Chaucer. These authors don't tell jokes, per se. Yet our modern humor owes plenty to their clever wordplay and sexually loaded double entendres.

* * *

One soldier said to another, "I had your wife without paying a penny."

The other soldier replied, "It's my duty as a husband to couple with such a monstrosity. What's your excuse?"

* * *

One soldier said to another, "Congratulations! You've got a baby boy."

The other soldier replied, "Thanks to friends like you!"

* * *

An Abderite saw a eunuch talking to a woman in the market and asked if she was his wife. The eunuch replied, "No, eunuchs cannot have wives."

"Ah!" the Abderite replied. "So she is your daughter?"

* * *

An Abderite asked the eunuch, "How many kids do you have?"

The eunuch explained he didn't have any balls, so he couldn't have any children. The perplexed Abderite asked, "When are you going to get the balls to have kids?"

* * *

Q: How many stoics does it take to light an oil lamp?
A: None. They just sit in the dark.

Q: How many pessimists does it take to light an oil lamp?
A: None. It's a waste of time since the new lamp will burn out soon enough.

Q: How many optimists does it take to light an oil lamp?
A: None. The sun will rise soon and it will be a bright new day.

Q: How many philosophers does it take to light an oil lamp?
A: That's an interesting question.

Q: How many gladiators does it take to light an oil lamp?
A: None. Gladiators aren't afraid of the dark.

Q: How many scholars does it take to light an oil lamp?
A: None. That's what scribes are for.

Q: How many actors does it take to light an oil lamp?
A: Only one. They don't like to share the lamplight.

Q: How many road builders does it take to light an oil lamp?
A: Five. One to light the lamp and four to lean on their shovels and watch.

Q: How many vestal virgins does it take to light an oil lamp?
A: Eight. Two to light the lamp, two to supervise the lighting, and four to watch.

Q: How many poets does it take to light an oil lamp?
A: A myriad of lyre-plucking singers stretching from the shining shores of Troy to Romulus's fair city.

Q: Do you know how many lyre players it takes to light an oil lamp?
A: No, but hum a few bars and I'll play along.

* * *

The philosopher wished to teach his donkey not to eat, so the philosopher did not offer his donkey any food. When the donkey died of hunger the philosopher lamented, "I've had a great loss. Just when my donkey learned not to eat, he died."

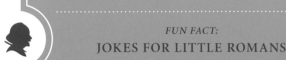

FUN FACT:

JOKES FOR LITTLE ROMANS

Q: Who succeeded the first emperor of Rome?
A: The second one.

Q: Where is Hadrian's Wall?
A: Around Hadrian's garden.

Q: What is a forum?
A: Two-um plus two-um.

Q: How was the Roman Empire cut in half?
A: With a pair of Caesars.

Q: What was the greatest accomplishment of the
   early Romans?
A: Speaking Latin.

* * *

A Thracian heard that crows live for more than a hundred years.
So he bought a crow to test it out.

* * *

Q: Did you hear about the Kymaean doctor?
A: He was operating on a patient screaming in terrible agony.
   So he substituted a knife that wasn't as sharp.

Q: Did you hear about the Kymaean house seller?

A: He always carried around one of its building blocks to show people what it looked like.

Q: Did you hear about the Kymaean who was swimming when it started to rain?

A: Not wanting to get wet, he dove down as deep as he could.

* * *

A man with bad breath looks to the heavens and says his prayers. Zeus scrunches his nose and calls down to the man, "Have mercy! You've got gods in the underworld, too, you know!"

* * *

Two soldiers are talking and one says, "Lend me a cloak to go down to the country."

The other soldier replies, "I have a cloak to go down to your ankle, but I don't have one that reaches as far as the country."

* * *

A boy ravished his grandmother during the night, and the next morning his father beat him severely for the transgression. The boy complained, "You've been mounting my mother for a long time, without suffering any consequences. Now you're mad I screwed your mother for the very first time!"

* * *

One pair of a twin dies. The other twin is walking through the market when a friend asks him, "Did you die, or was it your brother?"

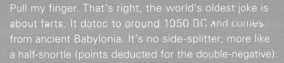

FUN FACT:
THE WORLD'S OLDEST JOKES

Pull my finger. That's right, the world's oldest joke is about farts. It dates to around 1950 BC and comes from ancient Babylonia. It's no side-splitter; more like a half-snortle (points deducted for the double-negative):

Q: What's something which has never occurred since time immemorial?
A: A young woman not farting in her husband's lap.

The ancient Egyptians had a funny bone, of sorts. These two jokes both date from around 1600 BC:

Q: What did the Universal Lord do after his daughter, Hathor, stood before him and exposed her vagina before his very eyes?
A: Thereupon the great God laughed at her.

Q: How do you entertain a bored pharaoh?
A: Sail a boatload of young women dressed only in fishing nets down the Nile and urge the pharaoh to go catch a fish.

One of the oldest jokes in English (predating Chaucer's ribaldry by a few hundred years) was handed down from the Anglo-Saxons in the tenth century AD:

Q: What hangs at a man's thigh and wants to poke the hole that it's often poked before?
A: A key.

* * *

A man told the philosopher, "Your beard is coming in now." So the philosopher went to the back door and waited for it.

Another philosopher asked what he was doing and, after hearing the whole story, said, "I'm not surprised that people say we lack common sense. How do you know that it's not coming in by the front door?"

* * *

A student visited the parents of a dead classmate. The father was wailing, "Son, you have left me crippled."

The mother was crying, "Son, you have taken the light from my eyes."

The student replied, "If your son were guilty of all that, he should have been cremated while still alive!"

* * *

A philosopher came to check on a friend who was seriously ill. When the man's wife said he had "departed," the philosopher replied, "When he arrives back, tell him I stopped by."

* * *

A mother with a sick child asked an astrologer to cast the boy's horoscope. The astrologer foretold that the child had many years left ahead of him. And then he demanded his payment.

The mother said, "I'll pay you tomorrow."

The astrologer objected. "But what if the boy dies during the night? I'll lose my fee."

* * *

A mother asked an astrologer to cast her son's horoscope. The astrologer foretold, "He will be a lawyer, a city clerk, then a governor."

The boy died shortly thereafter, and the distraught mother confronted the astrologer. "My son is dead. You said he was going to be a lawyer, a clerk, and a governor!"

"Madame," the astrologer replied, "had he lived, he would have been all of those things."

* * *

An astrologer cast a man's horoscope and said, "Sir, you are unable to have children."

The man objected, "But astrologer, I have five children already."

The astrologer replied, "Look after them well."

* * *

A man far from home asked an astrologer how his family was faring. "Everyone is fine, especially your father," the astrologer said.

"But my father has been dead ten years!" the man exclaimed.

The astrologer scolded, "Sir, you have no clue who your real father is."

* * *

Q: What did the shopkeeper say when he found a policeman having sex with his wife?
A: "I got something I wasn't bargaining for."

Q: Why did the man put his wife up for sale, tax-free?
A: So the tax authorities would impound her.

Q: What's the cleanest leaf among all other leaves?

A: Holly leaves, for nobody will wipe his ass with them.

* * *

PETRUCCIO: Come, come, you wasp, i' faith you are too angry.

KATHERINE: If I be waspish, best beware my sting.

PETRUCCIO: My remedy is then to pluck it out.

KATHERINE: Ay, if the fool could find where it lies.

PETRUCCIO: Who knows not where a wasp does wear his sting?
In his tail.

KATHERINE: In his tongue.

PETRUCCIO: Whose tongue?

KATHERINE: Yours, if you talk of tales, and so farewell.

PETRUCCIO: What, with my tongue in your tail?

—*TAMING OF THE SHREW*

* * *

DEMETRIUS: Villain, what hast thou done?

AARON: That which thou canst not undo.

CHIRON: Undo? Thou hast undone our mother!

AARON: Villain, I have done thy mother.

—*TITUS ANDRONICUS*

* * *

HAMLET: Lady, shall I lie in your lap?

OPHELIA: No, my lord.

HAMLET: I mean my head upon your lap?

OPHELIA: Ay, my lord.

HAMLET: Do you think I meant country matters?

OPHELIA: I think nothing, my lord.

HAMLET: That's a fair thought to lie between maids' legs.

OPHELIA: What is, my lord?

HAMLET: No thing.

—*HAMLET*

⚘ ⚘ ⚘

This Nicholas anon leet fle a fart
As greet as it had been a thonder-dent,
That with the strook he was almoost yblent;
And he was redy with his iren hoot,
And Nicholas amydde the ers he smoot.

"Now herkneth," quod the Millere, "alle and some!
But first I make a protestacioun
That I am dronke; I knowe it by my soun
And therfore if that I mysspeke or seye,
Wyte it the ale of Southwerk, I you preye."

—*THE CANTERBURY TALES*

✳ ✳ ✳

Shakespeare walks into a bar. The bartender looks up and says,
"Hey, you can't come in here! You're bard."

Jokes for Kids

* * * * * * * * * * * * * * *

Jokes for Kids

YOUNG CHILDREN ARE INCREDIBLY LITERAL-MINDED. Psychologists say that kids don't fully appreciate jokes until age five or six. By the time kids turn seven or eight they're often infatuated with knock knock jokes and Mad Lib–style word games.

This ability for kids to process jokes is—for some unexplained but well-documented reason—tied to lying: kids must first learn to lie, or at least understand what lies are and how to tell them successfully. Lying, it seems, lays the mental groundwork for processing the incongruity and subtleties of the grown-up world (and this should make us adults feel really crappy about the grown-up world we've constructed!).

It's unfair to write off the jokes in this chapter as mere silliness. Sure, these kid jokes *are* silly. Yet plenty of structured learning is taking place beneath the surface. Think of this chapter as a lesson in wordplay, metaphor, and puzzle-solving for youngsters.

* * *

Q: What did one ocean say to the other ocean?
A: Nothing. They just waved.

Q: What lies at the bottom of the ocean and twitches?
A: A nervous wreck.

Q: What happened when the red ship and blue ship collided in the ocean?
A: They were both marooned.

Q: What kind of ship never sinks?
A: Friendship.

Q: What did the fish say when he swam into the wall?
A: Ouch.

Q: What did the second fish say when he swam into the wall?
A: Damn.

Q: Why are some fish at the bottom of the ocean?
A: Because they dropped out of school.

Q: Why do fish live in salt water?
A: Because pepper makes them sneeze.

Q: Why did the teacher jump into the lake?
A: She wanted to test the waters.

Q: What do you get if you cross a lake with a leaky boat?
A: About halfway.

Q: Why do birds fly south for the winter?
A: It's easier than walking.

Q: Why do seagulls fly over the sea?
A: Because if they flew over the bay they'd be bagels.

Q: What kind of shorts do clouds wear?
A: Thunderware.

Q: Why did the man put his money in the freezer?
A: He wanted cold hard cash.

Q: Where do snowmen keep their money?
A: In snow banks.

Q: What do you get when you cross a snowman with a vampire?
A: Frostbite.

Q: Where do Chinese vampires come from?
A: Fanghai.

Q: Who brings monsters their babies?
A: Frankenstork.

Q: What do you call a witch who lives by the sea?
A: A sandwitch.

Q: What do you call a witch who lives by the sea but won't go into the water?
A: A chicken sandwitch.

* * *

Two goldfish were swimming in a tank, when one said to the other, "Hey, do you know how to drive this thing?"

* * *

Q: Why did the turkey cross the road?
A: To prove he wasn't a chicken.

Q: Why didn't the chicken cross the road?
A: Because he was a chicken.

Q: Why did the dinosaur cross the road?
A: Because the chicken joke wasn't invented yet.

Q: What dog keeps the best time?
A: A watch dog.

Q: How can you tell it's been raining cats and dogs?
A: When you nearly step in a poodle.

Q: Why wouldn't the lobster share his toys?
A: Because he was shellfish.

Q: What goes 99-clomp, 99-clomp, 99-clomp?
A: A centipede with a wooden leg.

Q: What do you call a cow with no legs?
A: Ground beef.

Q: What do cows make during an earthquake?
A: Milkshakes.

Q: What do you call a cow that won't give milk?
A: A milk dud.

Q: What do you call a cow that won't give milk?
A: An udder failure.

Q: What do you get when you cross a cow and a duck?
A: Milk and quackers.

Q: What did the duck say to the store clerk?
A: Just put it on my bill.

Q: What's invisible and smells of worms?
A: Bird farts.

Q: What birds spend all their time on their knees?

A: Birds of prey.

Q: What's green and pecks on trees?
A: Woody Wood Pickle.

Q: Why don't penguins fly?
A: Because they can't afford plane tickets.

Q: Why do birds fly south for the winter?
A: Because it's too far to walk.

Q: What do cats have for breakfast?
A: Mice Crispies.

Q: What happened when the cat ate a ball of wool?
A: She had mittens.

Q: Why do bees have sticky hair?
A: Because they use honeycombs.

Q: What's a wok?
A: Something you throw at a wabbit.

Q: Why did the elephant eat the candle?
A: He wanted a light snack.

Q: What do you get if you cross an elephant and a rhino?
A: Elephino.

Q: Why do ducks have webbed feet?
A: To stamp out fires.

Q: Why do elephants have flat feet?
A: To stamp out burning ducks.

Q: Why do gorillas have big nostrils?
A: Because they have big fingers.

Q: What do you call a sleeping bull?

A: A bulldozer.

Q: What do you call a sleeping dinosaur?
A: A dinosnore.

Q: What happened when the lion ate the clown?
A: He felt funny.

Q: Why did the frog make so many mistakes?
A: He jumped to the wrong conclusions.

Q: What is red and green and goes a hundred miles per hour?
A: A frog in a blender.

Q: What kind of shoes do frogs wear?
A: Open toad.

Q: What do you get crossing a teddy bear with a pig?
A: A teddy boar.

Q: What do you call an ant that prefers to be alone?
A: Independant.

Q: What is black and white and pink all over?
A: An embarrassed zebra.

* * *

A panda walked into a restaurant, ordered a meal, and ate it. When the waiter asked if the panda wanted anything else, the panda pulled out a gun, shot the waiter, and started to leave. The manager cried out, "Mr. Panda, you can't just shoot my waiter and leave like that!"

The panda replied, "Of course I can. Go look up 'panda' in the dictionary."

So the manager ran back to his deck and grabbed a dictionary. Under the entry for "panda" he read: "An animal native to China that eats shoots and leaves."

* * *

Q: What's the difference between broccoli and boogers?
A: Kids won't eat broccoli.

Q: Why did the tomato turn red?
A: It saw the salad dressing.

Q: What did the tomato do after falling behind in the race?
A: Ketchup.

Q: What did the grape do when he got stepped on?
A: He let out a little wine.

Q: Where do burgers like to dance?
A: A meatball.

Q: What kind of plates do they use on Venus?
A: Flying saucers.

Q: Why did the cookie go to the hospital?
A: It felt crummy.

Q: Why did the orange go to the hospital?
A: It wasn't peeling well.

Q: What do you call cheese that isn't yours?
A: Nacho cheese.

Q: When do you stop at green and go at red?
A: When you're eating a watermelon.

Q: Why did the little strawberry cry?
A: Because her parents were in a jam.

Q: What do you get if you cross a jet with a burger?
A: Very fast food.

Q: What did the hamburger name his daughter?
A: Patty.

Q: How did the hamburger introduce his daughter?
A: Meet Patty.

＊ ＊ ＊

One day a baby turtle was climbing up a tree. After a few hours
he reached the top, jumped into the air waving his front legs, and
crashed to the ground!

After recovering, he slowly climbed the tree again, jumped, and
once again crashed to the ground.

The turtle tried again and again, while two birds sat on a branch
watching him. Finally, the mama bird chirped to the papa bird,
"Honey, I think it's time we tell him he's adopted."

＊ ＊ ＊

Q: What would happen if you cut off your left side?
A: You'd be all right.

Q: How do you make a bandstand?
A: Take away their chairs.

Q: What has four legs but can't walk?
A: A table.

Q: What has one head, one foot, and four legs?
A: A bed.

Q: What has four wheels and flies?
A: A garbage truck.

Q: When is a car not a car?

A: When it turns into a driveway.

Q: Did you hear the joke about the roof?
A: Never mind, it's over your head.

Q: Why was the broom late to school?
A: Because he overswept.

Q: Why did nose not want to go to school?
A: He was tired of getting picked on.

Q: Why can't your nose be twelve inches long?
A: Because then it'd be a foot.

Q: What did one wall say to the other wall?
A: I'll meet you at the corner.

Q: What did one elevator say to the other elevator?
A: I think I'm coming down with something.

Q: What did one toilet say to the other toilet?
A: You look a little flushed.

* * *

A little boy walks into a barbershop. The barber whispers to his customer, "This is the world's dumbest kid. Watch and I'll prove it to you."

The barber puts a dollar bill in one hand and two quarters in the other, then asks the little boy, "Hey kid, which do you want?"

The boy takes the quarters and leaves.

"What did I tell you?" said the barber. "The kid never learns!"

Later the customer sees the little boy eating an ice cream and says, "Hey, little boy, why do you always take the quarters instead of the dollar bill?"

The boy licked his cone and answered, "Because the day I take the dollar, the game is over."

* * *

Q: Why did the boy eat his homework?
A: Because his teacher said it was a piece of cake.

Q: Why did the music teacher need a ladder?
A: To reach the high notes.

Q: How did the music teacher get locked in the classroom?
A: His keys were inside the piano.

Q: How do you get straight As?
A: Use a ruler.

Q: Why didn't the two 4s want dinner?
A: Because they already 8.

Q: Why did the teacher wear sunglasses?
A: Because his class was so bright.

Q: Why were the teacher's eyes crossed?
A: She couldn't control her pupils.

Q: What do you call a small river that runs into the Nile?
A: Juvenile.

Q: Why is the Mississippi an unusual river?
A: Because it has four i's but can't see.

Q: How did the Vikings send secret messages?
A: By Norse code.

Q: Who invented fractions?
A: Henry the ¼th.

Q: Who made King Arthur's round table?
A: Sir Cumference.

Q: What is the fruitiest subject at school?
A: History, because it's full of dates.

Q: Where did the general keep his armies?
A: Up his sleevies.

Q: Why did the golfer wear two pairs of pants?
A: In case he got a hole in one.

Q: What did the tie say to the hat?
A: You go on ahead, I'll hang around.

Q: Why did the little boy put lipstick on his head?
A: He wanted to make up his mind.

Q: How do crazy people walk through the forest?
A: On the psychopath.

Q: What do prisoners use to call each other?
A: Cell phones.

* * *

Knock knock.
Who's there?
Cows.
Cows who?
No they don't, they moo!

* * *

Knock knock.
Who's there?
A boy who can't reach the doorbell.

* * *

Knock knock.
Who's there?
Beets.
Beets who?
Beets me!

* * *

Knock knock.
Who's there?
Repeat.
Repeat who?
Who who who.

* * *

Knock knock.
Who's there?
Ice cream!
Ice cream who?
Ice cream if you don't let me in!

* * *

Knock knock.
Who's there?
Nobel.
Nobel who?
No bell, that's why I knocked!

* * *

Knock knock.
Who's there?
Tom.
Tom who?
Tom on, you know who I am!

* * *

Knock knock.
Who's there?
Howard.
Howard who?
Howard I know?

* * *

Knock knock.
Who's there?
Lettuce.
Lettuce who?
Lettuce in, it's cold outside.

* * *

Knock knock.
Who's there?
Canoe.
Canoe who?
Canoe come out to play?

* * *

Knock knock.
Who's there?
Arthur.
Arthur who?
Arthur more cookies in the jar?

* * *

Knock knock.
Who's there?
Honeycomb.
Honeycomb who?
Honeycomb your hair!

* * *

Knock knock.
Who's there?
Honeybee.
Honeybee who?
Honeybee a dear and hand me the magazine.

* * *

Knock knock.
Who's there?
Rita.
Rita who?
Rita book, you might learn something.

* * *

Knock knock.
Who's there?
Justin.
Justin who?
Just in time for dinner!

* * *

Knock knock.
Who's there?
Gorilla.
Gorilla who?
Gorilla me a hamburger, I'm hungry.

* * *

Knock knock.
Who's there?
Banana!
Banana who?
Banana split so ice creamed!

* * *

Knock knock.
Who's there?
Banana.
Banana who?
Knock knock.
Who's there?
Banana.
Banana who?

Knock knock.
Who's there?
Orange.
Orange who?
Orange you glad I didn't say banana?

* * *

Knock knock.
Who's there?
Boo.
Boo hoo?
Don't cry. It's only a joke.

* * *

Knock knock.
Who's there?
Anita.
Anita who?
Anita Kleenex. Ah-choo! Too late.

* * *

Knock knock.
Who's there?
Heaven.
Heaven who?
Heaven you heard enough of these awful knock knock jokes?

* * * * * * * * * * * * * * * *

ADDENDUM:
Worst Jokes Ever

* * * * * * * * * * * * * * * *

Worst Jokes Ever

THE DUMBEST, STUPIDEST, MOST OFFENSIVE JOKES EVER

Maybe you've heard of the "cutting room floor"? It's a phrase describing where discarded scenes from movies end up: literally on the floor after being edited out of a film. It's an apt metaphor for this chapter of unloved and unwanted jokes. If this book were a television show, we'd call them bloopers. If this book were a DVD, we'd call them "extras." No matter what you call them, these are jokes that didn't make it—officially, at least—into the *Ultimate Book of Jokes*.

Why not? Well, let's be honest: many of these jokes stink. In some cases they're so *not* funny that they may actually make you laugh. In other cases the jokes are on the wrong side of offensive and may also make you laugh—despite yourself.

We make no promises about, or apologies for, these cutting room floor jokes. If you have a low tolerance for stupidity and offensiveness, well, at least you've been warned.

NOT QUITE FUNNY

A woman has twins and gives them up for adoption. One goes to a family in Egypt and is named Amal. The other goes to a family in Spain and is named Juan.

Years later, Juan sends a picture of himself to his birth mom. Touched, she tells her husband that she wished she also had a picture of Amal. "But they're twins," her husband replies, "and if you've seen Juan, you've seen Amal."

* * *

Q: What's brown and sticky?
A: A twig.

Q: What's the friendliest school?
A: Hi school.

Q: Why does a chicken coop have only two doors?
A: Because if it had four it would be a sedan.

Q: Where do books eat dinner?
A: At the table of contents.

Q: What do you call a video of pedestrians?
A: Footage.

Q: What do you call a fish with no eyes?
A: A fsh.

Q: What's the difference between a teacher and a train?
A: A teacher makes you spit out your gum, a train tells you to choo choo choo.

Q: What did the man say when the picture fell on his head?
A: "I've been framed."

Q: Why was it so hot at the end of a baseball game?
A: Because all the fans left.

* * *

A man came round in hospital after a serious accident. He screamed, "Doctor, doctor, I can't feel my legs!"

The doctor replied, "I know you can't, I've cut off your arms."

* * *

Two Irishmen walk past a bar.

* * *

Q: Why are there only 238 beans in Irish chili?
A: Because just two more makes it two-farty.

* * *

I walked into a supermarket and saw a man and a woman wrapped in a barcode. I said, "Are you two an item?"

* * *

So these two muffins are in an oven. They're both sitting, just chilling and getting baked. And one of them yells, "God damn, it's hot in here!"

And the other muffin replies, "Holy shit, a talking muffin!"

* * *

Knock knock.
Who's there?
Opportunity.
It can't be, because opportunity doesn't knock twice.

* * *

A dog walked into a telegram office, took out a blank form, and wrote: Woof. Woof. Woof. Woof. Woof. Woof. Woof.

The clerk examined the paper and told the dog: "There are only seven words here. You could send another 'Woof' for the same price."

The dog replied, "But that would make no sense at all."

* * *

Q: Where do you go when your hand falls off?
A: To the secondhand store.

Q: Did you hear about the persistent raver?
A: He wouldn't techno for an answer.

Q: What's black and white and red and has trouble getting through a revolving door?
A: A nun with a spear through her head.

Q: How many Zen Buddhists does it take to change a lightbulb?
A: Tree falling in the forest.

Q: What kind of bees give you milk?
A: Boobees.

* * *

A group of chess masters checked into a hotel and were standing in the lobby discussing their recent tournament victories. Eventually the manager came over and asked them to leave. "But why?" they asked.

"Because," the manager said, "I can't stand chess nuts boasting in an open foyer."

THE WORLD'S LONGEST JOKE
(IS NOT FUNNY)

I really can't include the world's longest joke here, even in the addendum. Why? Because the joke is more than 11,000 words long and would stretch (by one wag's measurement) to 125 feet long if you wrote it all out on toilet paper.

You'll find the joke on multiple Web sites. Do a search for "World's Longest Joke" and you're sure to find it. Www.longestjokeintheworld.com is a Web site you can also go to.

SPOILER ALERT: I am going to give away the punch line, to give you a flavor of what it's all about. Giving away the punch line (if you can call it that) may be blasphemy to hardcore joke connoisseurs. However, in my opinion, the world's longest joke is not a joke. It's a short story with a crappy punch line. So I don't mind making a few enemies.

The RV got to the bottom of the dune, sliding at an amazing speed in the sand. Just before they reached the stone Jack looked across to check that they were still heading for the lever. They were. But Jack noticed something else that he hadn't seen from the top of the dune. Nate wasn't wrapped around the lever. He was off to the side of the lever, but still on the stone, waiting for them. The problem was, he was waiting on the same side of the lever that Jack had picked to steer toward to avoid the lever. The RV was already starting to drift that way a little in its mad rush across the sand and there was no way that Jack was going to be able to go around the lever to the other side.

Jack had an instant of realization. He was going to have to either hit the lever or run over Nate. He glanced over at Sammy and saw that Sammy realized the same thing.

Jack took a firmer grip on the steering wheel as the RV ran up on the stone. Shouting to Sammy as he pulled the steering wheel, "Better Nate than lever," he ran over the snake.

THE WORLD'S SHORTEST JOKES

A few candidates for the world's shortest joke:

1) Velcro, what a rip-off.

2) Midget shortage.

3) Stationary store moves.

4) Pretentious? Moi?

* * *

A man said to a woman, "You remind me of a pepper-pot."

She replied, "I'll take that as a condiment."

* * *

A man and wife are in tough financial straits, they're broke, and they need money. So they decide the wife will become a hooker. She's not quite sure what to do, so her husband says, "Stand in front of that bar and pick up any well-dressed guy who walks out. Tell him you charge a hundred bucks. If you got a question, I'll be parked around the corner."

After a few minutes a well-dressed man walks out of the bar and she smiles suggestively. He asks, "How much?"

She says, "A hundred dollars."

He says, "All I got is forty bucks on me."

She says, "Hang on!" and runs around the corner to her husband. "What should I offer for forty bucks?"

"A hand job," the husband replies.

She runs back and tells the guy all he gets for forty dollars is a hand job. He agrees. She gets in the car. He unzips his pants and exposes a rather large penis. She stares at it for a minute, and then says, "I'll be right back."

She runs back to her husband and asks, "Can you loan this guy sixty bucks?"

LAUGH, AND GO STRAIGHT TO HELL

Q: What did one saggy boob say to the other saggy boob?
A: If we don't get some support soon, people are going to think we're nuts.

Q: What do you say to a woman with no arms and no legs?
A: Nice tits.

Q: What's the difference between a Catholic priest and a pimple?
A: A pimple waits until puberty before coming on your face.

Q: What's the worst thing about screwing a three-year-old?
A: Getting blood on your clown suit.

Q: What do turtles and pedophiles have in common?
A: They both want to get there before the hair does.

Q: What do you get by crossing a rooster with a jar of peanut butter?
A: A cock that sticks to the roof of your mouth.

Q: What's the difference between jam and marmalade?
A: You can't marmalade a cock up somebody's ass.

* * *

I hired a midget hooker last night. I gave her ten bucks to go up on me.

* * *

I asked a midget for a dollar and he said, "Sorry, I'm a little short."

* * *

Mommy, Mommy, where do babies come from?

From storks.

But Mommy, who fucks storks?

DEAD BABY JOKES—
LOVE TO HATE THEM

Q: How do you know when a baby is a dead baby?
A: The dog plays with it more.

Q: What present do you get for a dead baby?
A: A dead puppy.

Q: How do you make a dead baby float?
A: Take your foot off of its head.

Q: What do you get when you cut a dead baby with a razor?
A: An erection.

Q: What's worse than ten dead babies nailed to one tree?
A: One dead baby nailed to ten trees.

Q: How do you fit fifty babies into a bucket?
A: With a blender.

Q: How do you get them out again?
A: Doritos.

Q: What's blue and bloated and floating in your beer?
A: A dead baby with fetal alcohol syndrome.

Q: What's brown and taps on the window?
A: A baby in a microwave.

Q: What's brown and gurgles?
A: A baby in a casserole.

Q: What's black and red and sizzles?
A: A dead baby on a barbecue.

Q: What goes plop, plop, fizz, fizz?
A: Twin dead babies in an acid bath.

Q: What's funnier than a dead baby?
A: A dead baby in a clown costume.

Q: What's funnier than a dead baby?
A: A dead baby sitting next to a kid with Down syndrome.

Q: How do you stop a baby from falling down a manhole?
A: Stick a spear through its head.

Q: What's white and red and hangs from a telephone wire?
A: A baby shot through a snow blower.

Q: What's red and is found in all four corners of a room?
A: A dead baby who's been playing with a chainsaw.

Q: What's the best thing about a Siamese twin baby?
A: Threesomes.

Q: What bounces up and down at sixty miles per hour?
A: A dead baby tied to the back of a truck.

ACKNOWLEDGMENTS

Scott would like to thank the following people for sending him jokes, most of which were very funny and appear in this book:

Teal Lewsadder, Jan Panyard-Davis, Mark Davis, Anne Davis, Paul Burke, Dominga Ramirez, Ramona Ramirez, Jane Panyard, Tom Panyard, Martha Panyard, Anto Howard, Fionn Davenport, Nathan Clapton, Amy Klinke, Ray Klinke, Kurt Hobson, Emily Hobson, Jane Rawson, Wendy Smith, Janet Austin, John Ryan, Jeff Trounce, Adam Davis, Barry Anderson, Rich Laos, Teri Laos, Michelle Hepler, Lela Hepler, Sydney Hepler, Jeff Lewis, Jacqueline Bennett, Kelly Gillease, Suzann Moore, Patricia Pagenel, Barrie Seidenberg, Scott Halstead, Katrina Sorhiakoff, Daniel Hackett, Jenny Crossling, Melinda Harrington, Alesia Stochel, and Jaime Fitzgerald.

Extra credit goes to the following people, for submitting jokes in quantity *and* quality: David Hepler, Jim Stanley, Bob Gross, and Lisa Reile.